T0318284

Strategic Security

Strategic Security

Forward Thinking for Successful Executives

Jean Perois

CRC Press
Taylor & Francis Group
Boca Raton London New York

CRC Press is an imprint of the
Taylor & Francis Group, an **informa** business

CRC Press
Taylor & Francis Group
6000 Broken Sound Parkway NW, Suite 300
Boca Raton, FL 33487-2742

First issued in paperback 2020

© 2019 by Taylor & Francis Group, LLC
CRC Press is an imprint of Taylor & Francis Group, an Informa business

No claim to original U.S. Government works

ISBN-13: 978-0-8153-5787-2 (hbk)
ISBN-13: 978-0-367-77905-4 (pbk)

Library of Congress Cataloging-in-Publication Data

Names: Perois, Jean, author.
Title: Strategic security : forward thinking for successful executives / Jean Perois.
Description: 1 Edition. | New York : Routledge, 2019.
Identifiers: LCCN 2018052811 (print) | LCCN 2019000041 (ebook) | ISBN 9781351123464 (Master) | ISBN 9781351123433 (Mobipocket) | ISBN 9781351123457 (Adobe) | ISBN 9781351123440 (ePub) | ISBN 9780815357872 (hardback) | ISBN 9781351123464 (e-book)
Subjects: LCSH: Leadership. | Executives. | Strategic planning. | Security systems.
Classification: LCC HD57.7 (ebook) | LCC HD57.7 .P4653 2019 (print) | DDC 658.4/7--dc23
LC record available at https://lccn.loc.gov/2018052811

Visit the Taylor & Francis Web site at
http://www.taylorandfrancis.com

and the CRC Press Web site at
http://www.crcpress.com

CONTENTS

PREFACE

Security has moved at a tremendous pace since I became a security practitioner a few decades back. The evolution and the complexity of threats have positioned new security fields on the front stage. Yet although I acknowledge the importance of these new developments that contribute to the security of goods and persons, and make it a more multifaceted industry, the principles that have guided security practitioners for a long time remain valid. I believe in the value of classical security.

If you were to ask me why a book on security strategy, I would answer that this book is not exclusively about strategic security. It is more about applying a strategic perspective to the work of the security practitioner. I will not please everyone by saying that being the best at their job may not be enough to make a successful career. This is the stuff we were told when we were children but our experience of life has often proved otherwise. Yet the reverse is also not true. Being bad at your job will not promote you either. The recipe is probably a mixture of competence—that comes with hard work—and of self-confidence. In this book, I affirm that if they want to succeed, security practitioners should also promote themselves in ways that some old hands would probably call self-serving. Yet there is no reason security people should devote themselves entirely to their organization, selflessly and to their own detriment, and be forgotten on the way up to promotion. Yet it happens and it happens too often. Somehow, security is part of these jobs that chief executive officers (CEOs) perceive as not really capable of evolution. We will discuss in the book the probable reasons behind this prejudice, because observation and experience seem to show that competent security professionals are often maintained at the level at which they were recruited, avoiding the humiliation of being mocked as the latest victims of the Peter's Principle. The idea of promoting a security cadre to a position of general manager of a structure, a facility, a plant, or a headquarters never seems to cross the mind of a CEO, while I have seen human resources (HR) and finance people be picked for the job and become CEOs or general managers of facilities or offices, while nothing qualified them over their security counterpart. Knowing finance does not make you a good manager any more than being an HR specialist make you an expert on industrial production. Finding a rational explanation for this disaffection is a complicated issue of which our profession is very much aware. Solutions are being sought in the academy, and the security profession is contributing to this much-needed effort at changing our image. Some say that by becoming more professional, security people will reach the C-suite and be chosen for more ambitious responsibilities at some stage. And they may be correct. However, the security professionals I have worked with were usually very professional, and no less competent in their field than HR, finance, or HSE managers. There seems to be a glass ceiling that security professionals fail to break through and I would like, in a modest way, to try to remedy to this situation. I hope that addressing self-help ideas and principles will help. For many years, I have read amazing books on self-development and often found them motivating and always exciting. Not everybody believes in their power. Which is normal since the power is not in the book, but should be found in oneself, and even so, I am not sure that this is what really matters. Self-development techniques bring a lot of benefits to the person who sets out to implement them with confidence, and I will discuss some of these principles, techniques, and processes in this book.

HOW THIS BOOK STARTED

This book stems from a course I wrote for the Security Institute UK titled *Strategic Security* for their security certificate quite some time ago. It was a short module that comprised eight chapters, complete with questions and small exercises.

It is only recently, after having left this course in the hard drive for a long time that I decided to have a look at it again and transform it into a book.

THE DISCOVERY OF SELF-DEVELOPMENT LITERATURE

The main difference between the syllabus and this book is that in the latter, I wanted to introduce the readers (or some of them, since the American readership is probably already familiar with the power of self-development techniques) to issues of self-help that have been the flavor of the day for a few decades, but really were pioneered in the first half of the twentieth century. How was my interest in these techniques aroused? It is an amusing story. I was the director of security for a major gas company in Qatar when I applied to go to a *rapid reading* course that was offered in Dubai. I was then completing my master's degree and thought that reading more and faster would help me to perform better in the doctorate program I intended to begin as soon as possible and in my work since I was, by nature, the chief threat analyst of the organization, and as such had access to several of the remarkable Jane's security letters. I thought that being able to read faster would be an advantage. Not that I was so busy in my daily activities, but I liked the idea of being a rapid reader. The course was very interesting and strongly delivered, but the real personal discovery was the support book used to test our increasing reading skills. It was a book by Richard Dobbins and Barrie Pettman titled *What Self-Made Millionaires Really Think, Know and Do,* and it introduced me to concepts I had never heard about. Let us be clear, my purpose never was to become a millionaire, or I would have not served in the military in the first place, and even less in the security industry afterward. Even today, it is not one of my targets in life. Like everybody, I just feel the need to have enough savings to end up my life decently, but consider everything above that to be a bonus. I am not sure that the authors of this book really believed that becoming a millionaire is the supreme objective of their readers. Professional acknowledgement and personal achievement seem to drive most of us toward personal contentment. To become a millionaire, one needs to love money, and I was not brought up with money as the supreme life value. Success and social position were more what my parents had in mind for their children and values instilled during childhood tend to stick, no matter what we claim or pretend otherwise.

This book, by Dobbins and Pettman, was a book of revelations, of sorts, and I read it at night in my hotel room with growing marvel. I discovered in it what I have since called the mental laws of success, which are a mix of principles and techniques to help one reach goals for career achievement. Simply written and absolutely sound in their logic, these "guidelines" somehow changed my life, or rather the way I was managing my career, something I had never really thought about until then.

Sadly, it was a bit late in my professional career to apply all of them to my everyday working life, and I lacked faith in the ultimate goal that I would become a millionaire, but applying them definitely improved the way I perceived myself and did a lot of good for my self-confidence.

What makes this book unique, therefore, is that it provides a mix of strategic advice about the way you should run your security department as well as recommendations on the way to manage your personal career to reap the benefits of your efforts. The security strategic thinking is nothing new. Several very good books have been written about strategy, and self-development books have sold by the millions, but this combined approach written specifically for the security professional makes it interesting. I am sure that many will find in it some recipes to set and achieve professional and personal accomplishments, and attain a fulfilling sense of satisfaction that makes life worth its while.

ABOUT THE AUTHOR

Jean Perois is a security practitioner working in the Middle East. He is a results-orientated security manager with a proven record of designing, developing, and implementing quality asset protection programs for major industrial projects in multicultural environments. His work experience includes expertise in strategic planning, business management, risk-assessment, security training, program development, physical security, force protection, security audits, and risk mitigation strategies. He is a security analyst with a passion for international affairs, an expert at monitoring security risks, and able to provide in-depth reporting on strategic issues and tools for decision making.

1

Thinking Strategically in a Corporate Environment

In ancient Greece, *strategoi* were army generals cum politicians, whose task was to run the internal and external politics of the myriad of city-states dispersed in the Peloponnesian Sea. The famous Pericles (495–429 BC) and also the great historian Thucydides (460–395 BC) were among *strategoi* who marked the history of the Ancient Greek world. The word means "army leaders," and these army leaders played a major role in the political life of the Greek cities in times of peace and of war. Their role was military as well as political, and it should therefore come as no surprise that the word led to the word *strategy*, first defined as the art of planning and directing military operations and then in a business context as a plan of action or policy designed to achieve a major aim.

In the security industry, as in any other branch of business, strategic thinking can be defined as the ability "to plan long-term while maximizing performance for the short term" (Bruce 2000: 5).

In this chapter, I am going to discuss the basic components of strategic thinking when applied to security:

- Understanding what strategy is;
- Analyzing your position;
- Planning a strategy;
- Implementing a security program.

1

UNDERSTANDING STRATEGY

A strategy is a *declaration of intent*, a statement of where you want to be in the medium to long term (traditionally the 5-year horizon is the minimum target). A strategy is important because it enables you to make sure that "day-to-day activities fit in within the long-term program of your organization" (Bruce 2000: 6). A strategy encourages everyone to work together to achieve common aims. Most companies have a strategic plan, but they often fail to communicate it to the lower echelons, where you are now sitting as head of security or security manager. As a newly appointed security manager, your first task will be to become acquainted with the strategic plan of your company.

Defining a strategy is an important first step. It has been said time and again that a security strategy must be in line with the organization's corporate strategy. However, if you have been given the opportunity to see a corporate strategy document, you know that it is extremely difficult to develop a security strategy from a business program! Security is traditionally conspicuously absent from business strategy documents and you are therefore left on your own to devise something that should not antagonize the projects and growth anticipated by the finance people at corporate level.

Strategy concerns itself with what will happen in the medium to long term. Five years is traditionally considered as the minimum target of a strategy, but really this decision remains your call. Day-to-day activities tend to take precedence over long-term planning, and this is fine, provided the long-term strategy does not take a back seat. Strategy needs to be communicated to all who need to know, both internally (the security department) and externally (the rest of the organization).

THE STRATEGIC PROCESS

There are three distinct phases to developing a new strategy: analysis, planning, and implementation. The importance of the first two cannot be emphasized enough, as I have noticed in my career that security managers are not often given second chances: you must strike right the first time. In order to do this, you must get the first two stages absolutely right (Figures 1.1 and 1.2).

Let us begin with the analysis of the current situation.

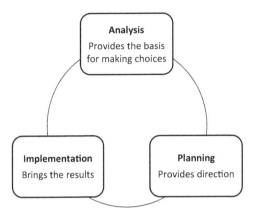

Figure 1.1   The strategy development process.

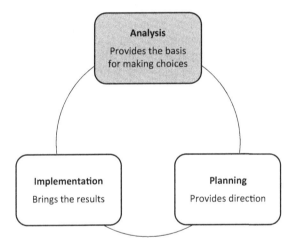

Figure 1.2   Stage 1: Analysis.

Stage 1. Analysis

Data Collection

To analyze data, you need to collect them first. It is important during this phase to collect as much information as possible regarding your organization and the current state of the security that is supposed to protect its assets (policies, plans, procedures, nature and number of tangible and intangible assets, etc.). Before you change anything in the security master plan, you need to understand what role security plays in the protection of your organization's assets (*people, processes, assets, and information*) and to understand what management's expectations regarding your department's performance are. You may want to know:

- *What characterizes the existing security in your organization?* Think first about the impression it projects to employees and to external observers. Is it discreet, overwhelming, sophisticated, with a lot of technology involved, friendly? What does it look like? What corporate image do security officers project: robust, friendly, well groomed, or could do better? Does the security in general (personnel, procedures, and technology) provide reasonable deterrence? How does it compare with security departments you have observed elsewhere or worked for in the past?
- *How do employees perceive it?* This is of course linked to the previous questions. And you generally cannot perceive quickly what employees feel about security. After all, you are their chief, and they will not want to be the ones who told you how unloved security people are in the company. The *shoot-the-messenger* syndrome is very much present in many organizations. It will be your job to observe—particularly during the 30 minutes during which employees and cars arrive at the company and reach their offices in the morning—to get a feel for the relationship between employees and security personnel. You can also sit in the lobby and observe the morning arrivals. This is always very instructive. Are people trying to avoid using their badges, are they friendly with the guards and receptionists? Can you observe piggybacking[1] or tailgating, or if you have been spotted, embarrassed behaviors?[2] What happens to the offenders, if caught? How do the security guards react, if they do? How do the caught-in-the-act offenders react? These small incidents always tell you a lot about the perception of security and the discipline of both the workforce and your staff.
- *What do you think the management expects from security?* This is indeed a very important question. It often happens that the new security manager does not meet the top people who know what they want from security. Apart from a quick, informal

discussion with the chief executive officer (CEO) or the general manager (GM), the security manager is often entering her office on Monday morning with not much clue about what is expected of her. There are several possible situations. One, it could be that you are the first security manager hired by the management. Ask yourself: Why is that so? What may have triggered this sudden need for more than a few guards managed by the facilities department? There may have been incidents; a merger with a more security-conscious organization may have taken place, there may have been a change in hierarchy or in priorities, etc. You need to get an answer to that question. Speak with colleagues at human resources (HR), health safety and environment (HSE) to get answers. It is important to understand whether you are here to satisfy an administrative requirement, or because recent events have created some anxiety in the organization's leadership. This happened to me when I was hired as the first director of security of the then biggest gas project in the Middle East in 2004. The project phase had been ongoing for 2 years, the construction of the gas plant was well advanced, and the pipelines were already buried underground or laid at the bottom of the sea when I was appointed. It took me quite some time to understand the numerous and complex reasons that motivated my nomination. Some were political, a few were technical, and most had to do with the complex relationship between stakeholders in the project and the relative and always changing balance of their power. And, as you most likely have already guessed, these stakeholders pursued different security agendas. All converged toward an end result in which the assets composing the gas project were to be secured, but each stakeholder had a very specific idea about what constituted assets, and the way they should be protected. Anyway, if you are the first security director in a project, sit back, observe, think, and brace yourself for a complicated future. There must be some serious thinking from your side about who you are going to serve—one cannot serve several masters well—and what is expected of you. This does not mean that you will do different things as far as your asset protection plan is concerned, after all, industrial and corporate security is a simple art, but internal politics will definitely impact the way you will implement company security policies, as well as how they will be prioritized and above all perceived. More importantly, you will have to think very seriously about the cultural aspects of security, and the perception of it by people coming from cultural backgrounds radically different from yours and those who often see security not as a bonus, but rather as a personal hindrance. You do not have too much time for this reflection. Do not forget that to establish yourself, you will have to implement some visible and tangible security measures quickly. Think that your appointment might have been a complicated issue, that some top managers may have had their own favorites, and that many people in your organization are far from convinced that a security department is a business necessity. To this end, I know that some of you will tell me that part of your brief, as security executive, is to educate management about what security entails, to help them differentiate between what is important and what is necessary, and I appreciate this commitment, but the reality is that management is usually very ignorant of what security is and that you will have to gain credibility before you have a chance to educate your hierarchy. And let's face it: Most of the time, they are not interested.

- *How do other competitors operate in comparable environments?* There are two ways to embrace this. (1) Your first possible approach is based on your experience. During the course of your career you may have worked in different environments and in different capacities. You have learned lessons and observed good setups and not so good ones. You have an intuitive feeling about what good security should look like and you can measure what you see according to what you saw elsewhere, that worked. (2) The second approach consists of measuring security by benchmarking what you see with what others do in the same industry. Doing this is sometimes easy, particularly when your facility is located in an industrial city, where neighbors operate very similar type of facilities in a shared environment. Chances are quite high that security meetings for security departments from the entire city are already organized to discuss threats, recent incidents, new trends and possible collegial solutions. Of course, it is a bit more difficult if you are new to the industry or if your facility is geographically isolated. For example, when I moved to my first assignment in the oil and gas industry, I had no previous knowledge of how security works in such environment. But the fact is that security, if it is never exactly the same, is based on the same premises, making environment learning quick and easy. To save time, befriend other security managers and ask if you can visit their facilities. Let them explain to you how their security program is organized. I have noticed that security managers with experience are usually very keen to show their setup and share their achievements with newcomers. Learn from others and never hesitate to ask; you will be surprised by how people are willing to help without hesitation. Later, when you are solidly established, never forget to return the favor.

- *What are the trends in the industry that could improve the security deliveries?* There is one safe—and I think it should be mandatory—way of evaluating the security posture of your organization: Perform a security survey as soon as possible after your appointment. Comprehensive security survey templates can be found in several books (e.g., Floyd 2008, Perois 2017) that propose specific or generic questionnaires that you can choose from depending on your industry. Perform a security survey of your company, headquarters, facilities, and warehouses; visit departments; talk to department managers; visit places; walk fences; and come at night, and you should get a feel for what security looks like in your company, plant, office, or headquarters. When this is done, you can write a report that will mark the starting point of your new security program.

    Then share this report with your team. Listen to older employees' explanations about the reasons flaws or obvious shortcomings were never addressed, why management considered some upgrades unnecessary or ridiculously expensive, and this will give you an idea about the probable willingness of senior management to support an ambitious security program.

    Before you dispatch the survey and prepare the plan, a SWOT exercise (see Figure 1.3 below) with your team is recommended. In Bruce's words: "It is a useful exercise that helps clarify the team's views, acts as a powerful *driver* of the plan and provides a way of measuring progress" (Bruce 2000: 26) (Figure 1.3).

Figure 1.3   The four components of the SWOT process.

Analyzing the Security Department Position

- Look at the security in your company from an observer standpoint:
  - Is the guard force proprietary or subcontracted? What does it look like, what message does it convey: authority? boredom? How appreciated does it appear to be? Are security incidents frequent and what is usually their outcome?
  - Are there tour guard systems? A lobby visitors' system? Or are we still filling out forms and exchanging signatures against a plastic badge? Is the procedure followed? Can some people get away with not following it? There is always a reason for security incidents and lax security and you must find the reason to address and fix the problem. Are security incidents recorded? Is it done electronically? manually? What happens to reports? Are patrol reports forwarded to maintenance—to report faulty lighting at night, for example? How long does it take to have lights fixed, if this happens?
  - Do they have vehicles? How do these vehicles appear? Are logbooks properly maintained? What is the procedure for filling up tanks?

- These are only a few of the myriad of questions that you need to pose and answer before you start looking for appropriate solutions.
- Examine the expectations from the management (more of this in Chapter 2):
  - Are you part of the weekly management meeting? If you are not, is your boss (usually a Vice-President [VP] collecting acronyms) part of it? Does she ask your help to prepare the meeting?
  - Does informal communication with managers show some special worries or concerns?
  - What do they believe needs to be protected?
  - Do you have access to your immediate superior easily? Is he a security man by trade?
- Study the relationship between the employee and the existing security requirements:
  - Do employees wear badges?
  - How would you qualify their relationship with the security personnel? Do they appear friendly? Do they appear to snub them? Are they aloof and/or a bit condescending? In return, what seems to be the officers' attitude? Do they look stern, good natured, cold, indifferent, rigid or relaxed but competent? Try to observe without prejudice, as if you were watching a film on TV. You may not be completely aware of this but this relationship will be one of the big missions of your new job. A security department trusted is a security department which is informed, which receives tips and which can do their work well thanks to a workforce who has confidence in them. If you fail to create this relation, your department will be blind and you will ignore what happens under your eyes. You will not be able to do the job you are paid for.
  - Observe at several days of interval, at slightly different times. Focus on small, apparently insignificant incidents: for example, is tailgating or piggybacking a frequent occurrence? Are badges often forgotten, or lost? Are offenders allowed to join their workstation? Are they given a temporary badge? Is any form filled or logbook documented?
  - Is there a clean desk policy in the organization? Walk the offices after hours and check flip charts ad white boards. Take pictures of them. Check whether confidential data are left on them.

- Are offices locked at night? Take a tour one night, and take note of what you see. Night-time security is always interesting. While you are at it, check offices, conference rooms, see if stamps are left unattended.
- Do deliveries follow some kind of procedure? How is the mail delivery system working?
- Assess the weaknesses in the security program.
  - Review the major security domains and check what is being currently done in terms of security and where you feel that there is room for improvement.
- Interview major stakeholders in your company.
  - It is important to establish a good relationship with other managers. You may be surprised by the accuracy of some of their remarks regarding security shortcomings. Managers have usually traveled and been exposed to many security programs. Their help can be invaluable in this regard. Do not let yourself be patronized but establish a relationship where *their* help improves *your* security programme.
- Interview both experienced and inexperienced security personnel:
  - What has been their training and professional experience, so far?
  - What are the possibilities of promotion in the company?
  - How motivated are they? How do they project themselves in the future? What do they think of their job?
  - What are their personal expectations, objectives, and even dreams? I have often noticed that security guards have dreams— often of training, of learning new skills, of getting certifications—that they only reveal to their line manager when asked.
- And of course, ask them how they think security could be improved in the company.
- Interview the leaders of the audit, legal, and ethics departments:
  - Obtain their views on the current state of security in the organization. In my experience, it has proven to be rather disappointing experiences, but one never knows. Security directors need allies wherever they can find them in the organization.
- Understand political issues at company level (this is particularly important when you work abroad).
  - If your organization is a joint venture, there are chances that different groups will try to influence or control the security department. It is important that there is a clearly defined chain of command, and that it is clear whom you are reporting to.

- Make sure that your strategic security plan is in line with the objectives of the joint venture (JV) and not of the companies composing the JV!
- Understand your customers (from the CEO down to the basic employee).
  - Security has, for the top management, a major public relations role, as it is often the first element of the workforce met by the visitor at reception or at the gate. Recently, organizations have put some serious efforts in having their security staff be more "visitor-friendly" than in the past. This aspect matters for your employers.
  - Try (hard) to look at security from the employee's perspective. Observe, but also discuss and inquire. Every organization has a history, and the relationship between the workforce always has its roots in the past. Whatever incidents happened, you must focus on establishing a harmonious (and therefore fruitful in terms of intelligence) and trustful rapport with the workforce.

In your strategic plan make sure that you plan for both the projected image of your security department and for the internal perception of it.

Assessing Existing Security, Skills, and Capabilities

In this phase, you will analyze what security, as a business unit, can do at present, and how their existing skills and capabilities may fit with the strategy you have in mind. Check the following:

- Policies and procedures (both at corporate and facility level)
- Security plan per facility (if any)
- Guards' post orders (if any)
- Security team: Are they old or young? How do they behave, how do they interact, how disciplined and tidy do they look, how friendly or unsecure do they appear, etc.?
- The presence of any system to measure security effectiveness (this can be all kind of metrics, key performance indicators (KPIs), etc.; for a better idea of what this can entail, see Chapter 4 about Measuring the Security Program)
- Access control in the morning, as well as parking behaviors. they are usually revealing
- Tour the place at night—all of it—this is usually illuminating (pun intended)

11

Define Your Scope of Work

- Define what needs to be protected. Assets need to be protected, but assets, tangible and intangible, may mean different things to different people. The top management has usually very precise ideas about what needs to be protected, but usually, they do not see themselves as being part of assets in need of protection.
- Evaluate the amount of protection needed. Think in terms of physical security, but also about manpower. There are needs for permanent features, and needs for special events. Check what can be subcontracted and what should not be subcontracted under any circumstances.
- Determine if your customers have any asset protection requirements.
- Are you contractually bound to provide specific types of requirements (there may be organizational, national or international standards to respect)? What are they? And what are these standards? Is the management aware of these requirements? (No, this is not a joke!)
- What do external and internal customers expect from you, the security program, and the security department? How do you think they perceive security tasks? Can you see a need for re-education and awareness for employees?
- Identify what is lacking in the security staff skills. See who has potential and who has less. Observe your people, and privilege enthusiasm and dynamism over anything else. To implement your program, you will need dynamic people to support you internally.
- Identify what is lacking in the current security program.
- Develop a list of projects to take the security program from where it stands to the level it needs to be to meet the organization's business objectives.

Establish a Charter for the Security Department

This item is often overlooked but has a major impact on your work and the way the security department will be perceived. It is strategic in that *it puts in place day-to-day processes that fit with the long-term objectives of the security department and the organization.* The list composing this charter can be as long as you want it to be, but here are a few extracted from Kovacich and Halibozek (2003: 134) that I find quite relevant for a majority of enterprises. This charter will list your strategic goals for the organization:

- Develop methodologies and implement processes to evaluate current security requirements and project future requirements on new business proposals and future contracts.
- Develop and oversee the implementation of a long-range (strategic is usually 5 years and beyond) corporate-wide security plan that details the efficient and cost-effective utilization of security resources.
- Provide overall management direction for all security activities within the company.
- Interface with directors of HSE, medical, audit, legal, and others as appropriate to resolve issues involving the security of assets.
- Provide a secure environment for the corporation to protect people, processes, physical assets, and information.
- Develop, implement, and maintain a company-wide security measurement system that permits evaluation of the effectiveness of each element of the security program.
- Develop corporate security policies to address the following security processes: administrative security, personnel security, physical security, information security, security education and training, investigations, contingency planning, security quality and oversight, fire protection, and international security operations.[3]

PLANNING: ELABORATING THE STRATEGY

Now that you have analyzed the trends in the business, understood what is expected of the security department, and have a fair idea of the competencies and shortcomings of your staff, you may start thinking about developing your strategic plan (Figure 1.4).

I believe that in practical terms, the first step for a security manager should be to create a security master plan for her organization.

The Security Master Plan

A security master plan is defined by Giles as "A document that delineates the organization security philosophies, strategies, goals, programs and processes" (Giles 2009: xix).

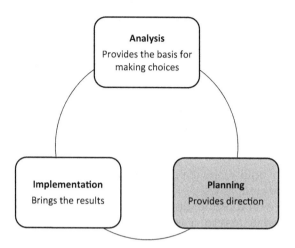

Figure 1.4   Stage 2: Planning.

The security master plan documents the security strategies of the business both for now and for the future. As I have already said, it is paramount that the security strategies are aligned with the strategies of your business. Yet, as previously discussed, the annual report will not tell you much in terms of security philosophy, this crucial element that should determine strategies, goals, programs, and processes. Often, security is not even mentioned by name in the annual business report. It will be up to you to develop a strategy based on what you understand to be your company's objectives.

Selecting the Right Security Program
Selecting the right security program means first establishing the framework into which the security master plan will develop. To do so, you need to define the limits of the strategic security master plan. A security master plan cannot encompass everything. This chapter will help you think strategically about the influences you need to consider when elaborating the security master plan structure and contents. It is not a guide to security master plan building,[4] which documents the security strategies both for now and the next 5 years. It is one way of organizing your thoughts and preparing a proposal that should enable you to gain the support of the executive management team, and open the way to the attached budget.

Understanding the Organization's Culture

The right security master plan will be one that fits the purpose of the organization's business objectives, but also one that best fits the company's culture. Dalton says, "To assure strategic success, the security manager needs to first understand the organizations' culture" (2003: 109). This is as important as the security needs because culture will orientate the work of the security executive and will determine which approach should be privileged for achieving success.

This point is even more salient when your company operates abroad with a multiethnic workforce and culturally diverse shareholders. It is best then to observe first, listen to experienced managers, and understand what will be and what will not be accepted before you rush into defining your security program. Get acquainted with the security history of the company. Understand the stakeholders' agendas, and guess how they will defend them. Imagine how this defense might collide with the security arrangements you have in mind.

Envisioning the Organization's Future

Once you have a clear idea of the limits of the future security program, your next task consists of understanding where the company wants to be in the next 5 years in order to prepare for adapted and relevant security solutions. To achieve this, you need to get out of the comfort of your office and meet people. Giles (2009: 6) suggests that you interview the appropriate executives of the company (chief operations officer [COO], chief financial officer [CFO] etc.) in order to know the following for the next 5 years:

- What growth does the organization anticipate?
- Do managers expect any product or service changes?
- Is an expansion or a reduction planned? Is growth expected to take part in existing facilities or will new ones be added?
- Are there overseas expansions and/or mergers in the pipeline?
- Are there any major layoffs or outsourcing activities planned?

When these issues of culture and future have been understood, it is now time for you to turn toward what you probably have been hired for: establishing a comprehensive security program for the organization, its affiliates, and its subsidiaries.

Elaborating the Security Master Plan

You have already worked hard on setting the framework for the security program. Earlier in this chapter, you learned how to establish a vision and mission statement, analyze the internal and external environments, and develop long-term objectives. This is quite an achievement. All this preliminary work provides a solid framework into which your security program will fit.

A word of warning, though: The security program you are about to produce deals with all aspects of security, from policies and procedures to technology and staffing. This is a vast scope. In elaborating the plan, think about two things: (1) that security is generally perceived as a cost center, tolerated rather than supported, and consequently, any change brought by security is usually poorly received and very much resisted and (2) that it is easier to try to fit the security program into the organization's culture rather than trying to change that culture. Remember that management sees you, as a person, as a cost center in a suit (at other times you might feel that they see you as a security guard in a suit!) and that most employees see security as people who restrain their freedom and complicate everything for the pleasure of making (really) regular people's life miserable at work.

Lastly, remember that to have any chance of success, your security master plan must be reasonable and cost-effective, and it must avoid both abrupt requests for change in procedures and expensive improvements in technology.

The strategic plan must take into account your psychological place in the organization, and you must serve your strategy with patience and discipline.

Formulate a Plan
It is now time to make decisions about what you want your security department to achieve and how you are going to take it there. You need to *formulate a plan* based on the data you have gathered so far (Figure 1.5).

The stages of the strategy planning are as follows:

Define your purpose: Create a statement of future goals, agreed upon with superiors, team members, and stakeholders. As previously mentioned, your purpose must fit with/match the strategic aims of other departments and teams in the organization. The statement should be kept brief and clear, concentrating on simple definitions of intent.

Set boundaries: Establish a list of what security actions you will focus on immediately and which ones you will put aside, at least for the time being. This is usually where you list the elements of your security program and where you say that you will deal with information security, but not cybersecurity, for example.

Figure 1.5 The six-phase plan formulation.

Choose strategic emphasis: This list will depend on three factors: (1) the priorities set by the management, (2) your feeling regarding the weaknesses of the security department, and (3) the changes that will yield the most spectacular security improvement at the lowest cost in the shortest period of time.

Estimate a budget: Even if you have no budget of your own and expenses are decided at a higher level of authority, it is always a good idea to try to put a figure on every change you want to implement. It will often have a strong impact on top-level decision making and protects you (*this is called company politics*) when the budget for a specific improvement is not allocated.

Integrate the strategy: Bear in mind that your strategy should not jeopardize other department efforts. For this you must identify and anticipate conflicts. Expect a lot of antagonism and resistance to any change brought by security. Be ready to compromise as you move along.

Remember: A security not accepted by the employees will not be implemented. It is as simple as that!

Communicate the strategy: This is probably the second most important issue after defining the strategy. You cannot expect people to embrace your strategy if they do not understand why this strategy is necessary and more importantly what it will do for them—the famous "What's in it for me?"

- Communicate your plan to every stakeholder, from the shareholder down to the employee.
- The methods can be varied and include: (1) detailed reports, (2) outline reports, (3) presentations, (4) newsletters and emails, and (5) online surveys.

Implement the Plan

The traditional stages of the implementation phases are as follows (Figure 1.6):

Prioritizing Change

Management, as previously mentioned, wants to introduce change, which is probably why they hired you in the first place, because of a feeling shared at the highest level that the current security posture is inadequate. However, *changes must also stem from your own observations*. As a security professional, you may already have noticed abnormal occurrences that escape non-professionals. Focus on these two streams of information, one coming from the management, the other one being the result of your observations. The following actions should be undertaken:

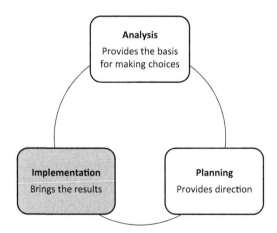

Figure 1.6 Stage 3: Implementation.

- Identify gaps in the current situation.
- Set priorities: Take your list of improvements and mark them as high, medium, or low priority. To do so, take into account the *impact* and the *urgency*. Handle high-impact/high-urgency improvements first!
- Draw up a list of issues that need improvement in order for the new strategy to succeed (Bruce 2000).

Planning Change

Bringing about effective change is vital to strategic success. To succeed you must:

- Define objectives, following the well-known SMART[5] rule.
- Allocate responsibility within your team, with the most experienced team member responsible for the relevant projects. Do not become the project manager, as you will lose the necessary distance to observe, redress, and encourage.
- Set milestones and reasonable time targets.
- Record progress. Designate an individual on the team to record progress, noting on a simple tool such as an Excel sheet any improvement brought to the plan, procedures, or post-orders.
- Involve the team. Create areas of responsibility. Make sure that the designated people are happy and interested in what there are supposed to do in implementing the program.
- Develop a culture of achievement in the security department.

Assessing the Risks

Your new security strategy will be met with resistance, no matter how brilliant and necessary it is. Anticipating this resistance and having a plan to answer the critics is part of the strategy itself. The more prepared you and your team are to face the criticisms, the better your chances are to overcome the threats.

The steps in this section are:

- Predicting problems with the team through brainstorming sessions and trying to find solutions to these problems.
- Assessing impacts of these threats to see how expected problems could impact the strategic plan. Assess the possibility that each threat will occur. Focus on *high-probability/low-impact* threats. Tailgating and wrong parking are high-probability/low-impact threats.

High-impact/low-probability events (1) are improbable although possible and (2) should they occur, would probably need a complete reassessment and restructuring of the strategy.

- Establishing some kind of contingency planning; in other words, thinking through alternative ways of achieving your strategic objectives should a major problem occur.

Review Operational Targets

As part of this strategic plan implementation you must establish operational targets for your team. You must agree with them on collective objectives but also on personal targets. To meet all the demands of your strategic security plan, skills and competencies will have to be acquired. In a period of financial scarcity, it is your existing team that will probably have to acquire and endorse those skills. Somehow this is a good thing, because this means a lot of training and skills acquisition, and this is fine because training is probably the greatest motivator of a security guard force. When you have established the skills needed to implement the program, transform these skills into training courses and assess which of your personnel should and could undergo such training. By doing so, you transform the strategic objectives of the department into individual targets. The impact will be huge. Do not forget yourself in the list of future trainees. If your department functions on a shoestring, do in-house training, walk-through talk through type. What is important is that training should become a regular function of your security program and that each training session, no matter its format, should be recorded.

As individual members reach their new skill target, the strategy will develop and provide for new objectives.

Motivate People

When one is in charge, one is elated by the power of duty and responsibility, and one tends to forget that others may not share this enthusiasm. *Members of a team need to be encouraged and rewarded.* They must be conscious—and proud—of the part they play in ensuring the success of the security strategy of the organization. The basic steps in encouraging people are:

- Listen to them and encourage suggestions *in a controlled framework.* Never forget that *you* are the boss. Bullies should not be allowed to win, and shy people may be full of brilliant ideas. It is your job to extract the best of your team members.
- Invest in training. Training is highly motivating. The lack, or paucity, of training is the most common complaint emanating from security

personnel all over the world. Training can be in-house and does not need to be expensive to be effective. *Reward through training.*

- Lead by example. Remember: When the chief stops, men and women sit down. When the chief sits, men and women lie down. You must be a beacon of enthusiasm and dynamism. It is not always easy, but who said it was? Enthusiasm should come with the responsibility. Amazingly, I have never seen enthusiasm written on a job description.

Monitor Performance

Performance monitoring is a complex and long-debated issue in security. Performance measurement is part of any strategic plan, and a strategic security plan should not be different in any way. However, measuring the effectiveness of security is not a simple task. How can you say how many attacks, thefts, embezzlements, or vandalism have been deterred by the presence of an apparent solid security setup? This is not an easy task. In consequence, security managers split along two attitudes. The first one is to say, "We are a cost center and there is nothing we can do about it." It is fine with me, but it may look a bit rudimentary as a justification for a manager sitting at the weekly management meeting with the other big COs and VPs (COO, CFO, VPs, you name it). The other attitude is to rely on metrics to show how important security is and the crucial role it plays as an enabler. I am, of course, a supporter of the second attitude. But it requires a lot of thought and effort, and it does not always convince. In other words, if you are serious about metrics, do not feel ashamed to look for help. We will deal with metrics in Chapter 4, Measuring the Security Program.

Monitor the Plan

A monthly meeting could be a good start to review progress. The purpose of this meeting would be threefold: (1) to review progress, (2) to resolve issues, and (3) consequently to review and realign strategy to maintain a tension toward objectives.

Be Flexible!

As a conclusion, I have to warn you that, whether you want it or not, you *will* be flexible. The strategic plan will come under attack from unexpected adversaries and at unexpected times. Alliances will shift and your supporters of today may let you down tomorrow (while the reverse is rarely true). Reasons are many and too numerous to list. Your team will be battle-fatigued at some times—it is inevitable. You might yourself lose stamina from time to time. Your management may lose interest in security and the threat situation may sometimes look so benign that your efforts will really look like futile gesticulations and wasted energy to others.

You need to adapt and be flexible to preserve the following:

- The strategic plan and its security objectives, which have been agreed upon by all, *at least in its spirit*
- The image of the security department, which is quintessential to the success of the strategic plan
- Your personal relationship with the other stakeholders, without which no success is possible
- Your leadership that is the key to success, yours and that of your department

Security does not operate in a vacuum, and you need to create a positive relationship with other managers. Your credibility is at stake. If you do not manage to preserve this relationship, you will not be supported in your efforts to impose change.

Creating, planning, and implementing a strategic security plan for your organization are heavily dependent on these factors. The human element is what will eventually make the difference between success and failure.

Be confident and persuasive, and do not try to achieve too much too quickly. Patience, it is said, is the mother of all virtues. And this is as true in security as it is in any other human endeavor.

SUMMARY

Selecting an asset protection plan appropriate to the needs of the organization is crucial to having security endorsed and supported by employees and managers alike. To be successful, the strategic security master plan must integrate the organization's culture and serve the organization's objectives.

The security master plan must be logical, relevant, and reasonable. The SMP will impact employees' lives, and, as with every change, it must be implemented gradually and supported by good communication and lots of flexibility.

MAIN POINTS

- A purposeful security master plan must serve the objectives of the organization while respecting and integrating its work culture.
- A relevant security master plan must address the major security issues of the organization and be cost effective.
- Success of the SMP implementation will depend on the relevance of change, its timeliness, its cost, and how it is communicated to the staff.
- Flexibility is not a weakness. Monitoring change is an art, and you will need flexibility to both preserve your image and reach your goals.

END NOTES

[1] Piggy backing is when an *authorized* person follows another authorized person in the facility without using the proper credential.

[2] Tailgating is when an *unauthorized* person individual follows an *authorized* person into an area.

[3] The full list of duties and responsibilities can be found in Kovacich & Halibozek (2003), pages 134–5.

[4] Another specific chapter deals with the elaboration of a security master plan (verify this information).

[5] **SMART** is a mnemonic to guide people when they set objectives, often called key performance indicators (KPIs), for example, for project management, employee performance management, and personal development. The letters broadly conform to the words Specific, Measurable, Attainable, Realistic, and Time-sensitive, although authors tend to take liberties with this mnemonic.

REFERENCES

Bruce, A. & Langdon, K. (2000) *Strategic Thinking*. Dorling Kindersley: London, UK.

Floyd, W. R. (2008) *Security Surveys*. ASIS International: Alexandria, VA.

Giles, T. D. (2009) *How to Develop and Implement a Security Master Plan*. CRC Press: Boca Raton, FL.

Kovacich, G. L. & Halibozek, E. P. (2003) *The Manager's Handbook for Corporate Security: Establishing and Managing a Successful Assets Protection Program.* Butterworth Heinemann: Amsterdam, the Netherlands.

Perois, J. (2017) *Getting the First Step Right: A Risk Assessment Guide for the Security Manager.* ASIS International: Alexandria, VA.

Strategic Business Planning & Implementation Course, Brighton School of Business and Management Ltd—Strategic Business Planning—© 2007.

2

Selling Your Security Program to the C-Suite

INTRODUCTION

In the previous chapter, we discussed what strategic thinking is about and how it applies to corporate security. We exposed the strategic process, and discussed the necessity, as early as possible, to analyze the department's position, assess the existing security posture of your company, define your scope of work, and establish a charter for the security department. We also examined how strategic thinking could be applied to selecting and defining the right security program, and why and how it should keep in line with the business objectives of the organization.

In this chapter, we will continue applying strategic thinking to the way you need to present your security program to the top management. This chapter will help you think strategically about the influences you need to consider, with the purpose of gaining support from the executive management team and obtaining the budget needed for the implementation of the program.

GENERIC EXECUTIVE MANAGEMENT EXPECTATION: COST NOTHING!

Kovacich and Halibozek reminds us that the executive management is responsible for the protection of all assets in the organization. As with every aspect of the business, executive management holds the ultimate accountability and responsibility for security. However, "how executive management defines a successful security program may differ significantly from how a security professional sees one" (Kovacich and Halibozek 2003: 95).

As a security practitioner, you will want to create a solid program, comprehensive with plans, policies and procedures, physical security, personnel security, administrative security, etc. Your objective is to reach compliance with accepted best practices—or existing standards if you have to comply with any. This is your job, what you enjoy doing, and you are naturally eager to create a secure environment for your co-workers. You think that risks should be controlled, threats monitored, and vulnerabilities addressed because you believe in Murphy's law, that if something can go wrong, it will.

Your hierarchy, though, might think differently. Security is at best a spurious concept, and at worst an impediment to solid dividends (for the shareholders) and solid bonuses (for the C-suite). All these people are interested in is money, which they call profit. After all, this is the reason behind any business enterprise, is it not? As a middle manager you may not always be conscious that your bosses, and particularly the CEO, are *not* reigning supreme above the company. They answer to a board which chose them on the promise to the investors that fat profits would be made and hefty dividends paid. As sympathetic as your CEO can be, she has targets to meet—targets that probably wake her up at night—and sees professional life through the prism of cost effectiveness. Her position is not always as secure as it may look from the middle of the pyramid where you stand. She normally chases unnecessary expenses, because her budget must be as lean as humanly possible to generate maximum profits for her employers. After all, if your organization was not making any profits you would not get a job at all. This is probably the most difficult concept to grasp for a security manager: this perception of oneself as a cost-center. As has already been said many times, security is the ultimate enabler: Without security, there cannot be any commercial activity, at least not in the long term. Yet, from managers at your own level up to the chairperson and CEO, all perceive security as a cost center. Although this perception could be easily challenged by saying that security creates the conditions without which the business cannot operate and that, for that obvious reason, it should not be perceived as a cost center but as a business enabler, it remains that this is not what people that count (the pun *is* intended) believe. If they could say it openly on the day they appointed you, their *orders* would hold in this simple sentence: Make us look good, be compliant, and cost nothing!

I will come back regularly to this tension between what is expected of your department and the reluctance of the C-suite to invest in security. If they agree that security must be led by an effective leader, what they mean by that is one who understands that security is there to serve the organization's (financial) interests. You have been chosen to be that leader: Do not disappoint!

What does it mean in practical terms? For the management, your brief is simple: Do not spend unnecessary money on security unless you can convince them that there is no other alternative. What it means for you in practical terms is that you must establish a balance between what you would like security to be—an unreachable goal—and what the management is ready to spend on it.

GAINING MANAGEMENT BUY-IN

As a junior practitioner, this problem may not be an immediate one, as it may take some years until you are the direct interface with the CEO or the VP of security in your organization. But it is nevertheless good that you understand how decision makers should be approached and do it with some self-confidence.

Dalton (2003: 18) insists that understanding the management's perspective is paramount. By understanding their motivation, you will be able to gain the support of decision makers, and come to be seen as their partners. The hook can only take one of three forms:

- If there is a demonstrated ability to solve the problem
- If there is provable benefit (such as promotion, cost savings, good will)
- To take the problem away from the decision maker ("relieve the pain"); when people are in pain, cost becomes a secondary concern; they just want the pain to go away and are willing to make a quick and positive decision

Let us see the issues in turn:

1. A Demonstrated Ability to Solve the Problem
   This signifies, of course, that there is a problem, or at least that your hierarchy feels that there is a security problem somewhere. Understanding its nature and magnitude precisely is the first task you must assign to yourself. Is there a security problem in this

company? Is this the reason behind my hiring? Is security itself the problem? Why? And second, how does the management perceive this problem? These may be two different sets of questions. As an experienced practitioner, you may have observed several worrying issues in the security department since your appointment. You have taken notes, and thought very seriously about ways to fix the different issues that hamper the good march of security operations. It is possible that these shortcomings were not even noticed by your hierarchy and it is also possible that they have hired you to do something entirely different than what you think should be done to improve things. First things first: If you want to be able to answer the CEO's questions, you must understand what the top management thinks the security problem(s) is/are. And you must put what you thought would be your fist tasks on the job on the back burner, or treat them as lower priority items.

In 2005, I went to a job interview for the position of security director of what was then a mega-project in the region. The way I ended up being interviewed was complicated and, to this day, I do not really know why I was summoned and why I was chosen. I did not realize this at the time, but there were other candidates, perhaps more qualified than I was, and I was picked because I was acceptable to all shareholders, in other words, the least controversial of the candidates. Surprisingly, my security capabilities were never even discussed. The interesting point in this anecdote is that I flew from Jeddah, where I was then working, to Doha to spend a day meeting the top brass in the project and to this day it remains one of the most interesting days of my professional career. Although I met the big boss only briefly I was then passed from deputy GM to VPs to the HR manager for individual interviews. I am still amazed by the fact that I almost did not say a word during this fateful day. I simply sat and listened to these important men. For almost a week I had rehearsed in my flat in Jeddah what I would say when asked the questions How do you see your role in the company? What are the first measures you are going to take to improve the current situation? What do you think the security situation is currently? and so on. Each person I met explained to me what was expected of me— by the acting CEO—as a security director and gave me food for thought about the way I would have to accomplish my task. What shocked me was that none had the same story to tell. All seemed to have quite a precise idea of what I should be, do, and change in the current security situation—each agenda being very relevant and acceptable, but each coming from a different perspective. One was envisioning my role as a high-level advisor to the acting CEO, a second one thought I was going to spend my time in hard-hat and overalls on site to make sure security procedures about access control and road traffic were duly applied, the HR manager was seeing me as the man who would hire consultants to do what I saw as my job, other VPs had really no clue and explained to me the project by lack of knowing what was expected from me. I flew back that evening with no idea of what my job would be, but convinced that I had the job. And I got the job!

This interview experience was illuminating in that I was suddenly confronted with the complexity of company politics in a multicultural organization, and I realized that security would have to be thought about on those terms. People from American and French oil and gas companies had completely different visions of security than did the locals who were slotted to run the show once the project turned operational. To sum up, none of the four top persons I met really considered my capability to fulfil the role—and they gave me the job without asking one question about my skills and capabilities. That was the first surprise. I had the feeling that the position was a bit big for me, and had prepared myself thoroughly by reading all available information I could put my hands on about *the perfect* or *the successful interview* so I could answer embarrassing questions that might reveal a relative incompetence and lack of oil and gas experience. My efforts were a complete waste of time. I looked the part and did not appear as like a potential threat or embarrassment to any of the partners, and that was enough. Both the VP of operations and the HR manager explained in broad strokes what a security manager should do and what the expectations of higher management were. The least that could be said is that there were almost no overlapping areas between the four portraits I was given that afternoon of the perfect security director.

2. Is There a Provable Benefit?
   This is a very important question and one that can leave you quite mystified. Security managers are not used to such terminology. We talk about threat, risk, vulnerabilities, and consequences, not about benefits, advantages, or added value. What this states, in reality, is that the top management will not back your security

program unless they can understand that there will be something in it for them—directly (a tangible advantage) or indirectly (an intangible benefit, often in terms of image or reputation).

Does this mean that they are only interested in security if it helps them fulfil their own personal and career objectives? Yes, it does.

Top managers are no different from the rest of us, except that they are more successful. And the reason why they are more successful is that they are focused on clear personal and professional objectives (more on this in Chapter 6). They see their every move and action in terms of personal benefits and career fulfilment. Disappointed? You should not be, because when you are done with this book, these are principles that you will also adopt to move your career to the next level. There is no other way.

Thus, there must be in your security program something that will benefit your immediate superior, your VP or your CSO.

How can a security program serve your hierarchy's interests?

Telling them that your security program will allow them to do business and make profits will not work: They were doing business and making profits before you joined and asked for this massive budget increase. You must really sit back and think. To start your thinking process, you must rewind the story and think about the circumstances that led to your recruitment and more importantly to your designation. If the position was advertised, there must have been a reason behind it. And behind every position there is a story. Who were the prospective candidates for the position? Were they direct hire or were they proposed by security companies? Why were you preferred? Has the process of your designation upset people? You need to know all this, because in the corporate world, for which I think few security practitioners are prepared, one needs to know where to find support and from where no support will come.

The second thing you need to know is what is or are the reasons behind the job. Is it a new job or did the previous security manager depart? What happened that triggered the decision? Are there new partners? Have unforeseen threats emerged? Have there been a few nominations at board level? Or a merger between companies? A merger is often a trigger for an assessment of the security posture of a project or of an existing plant. The designation of a security director may be at the request of one of the parties. You must know which one, because this one should be your natural ally. You must also know who objected to creating (1) the position and (2) your designation, because this party will be very critical of your efforts and it is now your job to convince them that you add value to the organization. Inquire about the debates that must have preceded this discussion. Most managers, who are now becoming your colleagues and like you because you are a nice person, were present when the discussion started, and possibly were involved in the discussion. They will let you know how it all happened. Knowing this will not make your task easier but will help you focus on the important people to keep happy—rather to make sure that you do not disappoint those who got you the job—and help you understand where criticisms will come from, whatever you may try to achieve. I know it has nothing to do with doing your job as a security manager, but believe me, it has everything to do with keeping it! In both cases, they are your action targets, because the rest of the management team very often does not care and will follow the flow. Then, for friends and foes, you need to show that your presence and your actions do provide some benefits—to the organization, and more importantly to the individuals who were instrumental in your designation. And in some way, you have to make sure that your actions do not harm those who did not want you and wanted the job for one of their protégés.

Times of crisis are ideal to make one's mark. If you happen to have been appointed during a period of serious incidents, this is very good, because you can relatively easily help your manager show her own hierarchy that she is controlling the situation and that a plan is ready in case of crisis (I recently travelled to South Korea to prepare a global security plan—including an evacuation plan—that I am sure reflected positively on the senior manager who had requested it). But nothing gets forgotten as fast as fear. Should nothing happen for some time, everyone up there returns to a condescending attitude toward security, and you immediately feel that your demands are not taken seriously anymore. In those periods, it is difficult to demand budget increases. This is as true of security as of almost any other department, but it is more worrying for security, because security improvements—particularly technical (electronic) security—need to be planned. In such circumstances, the onus is on you, and your creative mind—to find way of improving apparent security and make sure that people notice.

I am not a big fan of the attitude of some security managers who think that security should be invisible and that good security is no apparent security at all. A colleague of mine, an Arab national, was absolutely fascinated when he visited with a group of VIPs the offices of one of the major French industrial company in La Défense area near Paris.

31

"Security was good, and we did not see anybody," he remarked. "We have too much security here." I understand his point. VIPs do not want to be bothered by security people. Fine, I can accept that. Provided that every VIP visitor has been previously vetted, is under constant CCTV observation, and is provided with a discreet but efficient escort! It would be pure madness to let VIPs enter a place without being 100% sure of their identities, and without offering them solid personnel protection. Yet, some people, for image and ego purposes, want to carry an image of normal person, liked by all, who does not need to be protected because they have no enemies. These VIPs are really a pain in the neck, and I had to deal with a few of their kind in the Middle East and did not enjoy the experience. To come back to my previous colleague's experience, he really liked the unobtrusive security and the fact that their delegation was stopped nowhere—what he ignored was that their security was monitored from one floor below, with constant CCTV and a full security and medical team ready to intervene at immediate notice. He tried to convince me that we should get inspiration from this example and get rid of a few security officers that do not add value. Notwithstanding the fact that deterrence is one of the functions of security, and that in some cultures, deterrence is a necessity, I had to explain to him that what he could not see was there, elsewhere, and that the officers at the ready and the mobilized personnel for their short visit were probably in numbers far superior to what we could put on the ground in our headquarters or in our industrial facility. No need to say, I wasted my time.

Previously, I have used the word *creative*. This is an important issue in security and I have dedicated Chapter 7 to this concept of creative security. As John Adair wrote: "Your task as a creative thinker is to combine ideas or elements that already exist, thoughts that hitherto were not thought to be linked, then you will be seen as a creative thinker" (Adair 2009: 7). In other words, if you cannot increase security costs because it is not the right time to do so—and it is almost never the time—you can reorganize security in a non-obtrusive and appeasing way that will cost nothing and that employees can appreciate. Somehow it is a creative approach. A softer security can appease existing tensions between employees and security, and your manager may be thanked for that by the CEO or any other individuals at the top floor.

What is important is to do something that appears to be an improvement, and that satisfies your manager. The other important thing is to keep track of what you are doing. Because security is so misunderstood by the C-suite, your VP must be able to tell what the program is, what you are doing, and where you want to go. Perception is of course everything. I remember that in headquarters where I worked, the security personnel were deployed in the morning between 7:15 and 7:45 to ensure a fluid flow of vehicles outside and of people inside the building and make sure that there would be no tailgating and other unruly behavior. After a few days of this quite reasonable deployment of people, the security manager for the tower was summoned by the general manager who told him, "We need to fire a few security people. There are too many of them. When I come to work there are security people everywhere and they are absolutely useless!" Saving the job of these security officers was not an easy task, but we succeeded, but for a while only.

3. To Take the Problem away from the Decision Maker
   This point is of course valid only when you have elucidated what the security problem that poisons your boss's life really is. If the reason behind your hiring is an acute security problem (continuous theft of equipment, fraud, drug issues, etc.) you must concentrate on these issues above everything else. The solution to this problem is paramount to your credibility and key to the budget you will eventually be granted. If you can, put the solution in a greater scheme that will open some lines of budget. A smuggling problem can mean equipment purchase, specific training, changes in policies and procedures. These are tangible and intangible actions that enhance the profile of the security section or department as well as your image. Thefts of equipment, copper wires, or solar panels in far-off places may lead to CCTV installation, operator training, a revamping of the patrolling system, or new equipment—all tangible actions that put security in the limelight and make it appear as a business partner. Security is normally poorly handled by the C-suite. As Green remarked in an email to the author: "Top managers seldom talk the language of security, few have tried to understand the true value of it and have taken the effort to understand its basis and ethos" (email 23 August 2017). The onus is therefore on you to take the problem away from the decision maker and bring it back, entirely or partly solved, to get your solution approved. Doing this requires skills and you may not be the best person to suggest how to acquire those skills. But they are necessary if you want to succeed and appear to your hierarchy as a real enabler!

MANAGING THE ANXIETIES OF THE
C-SUITE AND THE ISSUE OF THREAT

Kovacich and Halibozek (2003: 96), in their very pragmatic approach, suggest that you always have some answers at the ready to potential security questions your hierarchy might want to and will ask:

- How much protection is *really* needed?
- When are the physical assets, people, and information of the company effectively protected?
- What are the risks and vulnerabilities for the operating environment?
- How are resources best deployed to achieve an acceptable level of risk?
- What tools and processes are needed to ensure an appropriately secure environment?

You notice that the word *environment* appears twice in these questions. It is therefore important that you highlight that security creates an environment susceptible to allowing business to thrive. It is important when you plead your case with management that you present your recommendations and/or propositions from a business perspective.

You must always recommend applied security rather than best-practice security. The business impact of security actions must always be considered. Of course, you will not convince everybody; however, a business-inspired asset protection program has a greater chance of being accepted by stakeholders. Business people tolerate the idea that security is the condition for sound and prosperous business operations.

You really have to ask two simple questions—What do we have to fear (apart from fear itself, I know)? and Are we ready?

These two questions can be split into several questions: (1) What is the nature and magnitude of the threat? (2) Who could want to harm our business and why? (3) Are there ways to protect against this threat at minimal cost? (4) How imminent is an attack? (5) Which forms could it take?

I have always noticed with surprise that it is quite acceptable to discuss security equipment purchases or change of procedures with top management, but much less acceptable to talk about the threat and try to define it. Of course, it is a curious behavior because the threat is what will make us adapt our security posture. And yet, in many organizations, improving the security posture is not linked to an update in the threat assessment. Why is that so? Why does the idea of discussing threats put executives ill at ease? Many of them will tell you, "You want more cameras? Ok, I'll get you the money." But discussing the threat is usually not acceptable, as if it were indecent talk. That puts you in an awkward situation in which you ask for more equipment, more training, a change of procedures, and more personnel to serve the asset protection program, but you cannot really discuss the reasons behind these requests. In projects abroad, the local element of the project, particularly at the top level, will perceive the mention of the threat (be it a terrorist threat, a criminal threat, or a disgruntled employee's threat), as somewhat offending.

When one has to deal with several equally important partners who are culturally distinct you need to tread very carefully. Never underestimate the political context of your situation. Weigh the power of all and sundry and think carefully where your loyalties should be. Managing security in big companies is a political exercise, and you must pace yourself slowly, all the time, to avoid creating animosity and antagonism between the partners and yourself.

YOUR ACCOUNTABILITY TO EXECUTIVE MANAGEMENT

Your job description says that you are responsible for leading and managing the security department as well as the security program of your organization. You are also responsible for achieving security compliance if your organization follows a standard of any sort (International Standards Organization [ISO], American Society of Industrial Security [ASIS], etc.) and for this you are accountable to your hierarchy. In fact, all these actions are the consequence of one main responsibility: Understand the level of risk that your organization is facing and once it has been measured against the risk appetite of your hierarchy, put a security program in place. From Kovacich: "It is your responsibility to work with executive management to establish an acceptable level of risk. Establishing an acceptable level of risk should take place only after threats and vulnerabilities have been identified, validated and analyzed" (Kovacich 2003: 97).

Again, this is easier said than done because you may encounter a managerial reluctance in many organizations, to discuss threats frankly and candidly. Somehow, managers think that threats need to be defined by specialists. I discussed threats with my managers many times in my corporate days and I always faced the same defiance. Who says so—meaning who are you to assert such thing? How can you assert this without being

35

a professional analyst? This of course was always a bit weird because the first part of any risk assessment is always the evaluation of the threat. It appears to many decision makers that only high-level think tanks or risk consultancies are capable of understanding and designating the threat. Yes, these entities have loads of very competent and experienced analysts, but these analysts traditionally analyze the government's situations. Private security companies deal with private organizations. And private security companies do have teams of experienced and competent analysts who seem to know the threats facing your organizations better than you do, even if you have been deployed on site for some time. This is fine with me. I have always advertised the merging of the jobs of security analysts and security consultants, because I think that in the private sector, they are moving on a converging path.

The consequence of this reluctance to accept your interpretation/ evaluation of the threat is that you may have to require the services of professional analysts (Stratfor, Control Risks Group, Exclusive Analysis, Aperio, and others) to make your position tenable and your recommendations acknowledged. It is often only when the external analysts have said that your company is facing threats—we are talking about terrorist threat—of course, that you will be able to advance your position. You may be in a situation where the terrorist threat is not what really worries the management, but my experience is that the other threats are—wrongly—not taken seriously enough. It may also happen that the management and the people in the field have completely different opinions on the threat. I remember visiting a big company on the eastern coast of Saudi Arabia, to perform a mandatory security risk assessment, where the site security manager's main concern was the theft of equipment and material that really made his life problematic. The idea of guys blowing the place up or poisoning his water—it was a water production company—seemed a very far-fetched story that he did not support. But he wanted me to recommend all sorts of physical barriers and more stringent procedures to make sure that the equipment under his guard would stop being stolen.

Anyway, once you have established what level of protection is required and incorporated in your program the risk appetite of your management, it is up to you to put together a total asset protection program (Dalton), also known as a corporate asset protection program (Kovacich).

You must now establish the security master plan, implement it by stages, and make it a success. You are the security professional and it is expected that you will think strategically to adapt your security program to the business objectives of the organization.

YOUR EXPECTATIONS OF EXECUTIVE MANAGEMENT

As much as executive management have expectations about their security manager, the corporate security manager can succeed only if expectations of the executive management are, at least in part, fulfilled. It must be known in the company that the executive management supports the security program you are building with commitment and steadfastness. When you can, make it know that the C-suite backs your program, and think about ways to implicate the CEO in the implementation of the security program. Prepare, for example, a "clean desk" policy, which is usually a good start—and there is always a need for it—and have it signed by the CEO and communicated through the company's intranet. You may, as I did a few years back in Qatar, invite a well-known security specialist to present a specific aspect of security that everybody will find interesting. I invited the Canadian world specialist on pipeline security, and he agreed to come because it looked to him like a potential platform to sell his courses and obtain contracts in the region. I used this opportunity to invite many senior managers in the company because pipeline security is a major concern in the gas distribution industry and they knew the boss supported the initiative, as did the ASIS chapter chair. This showed a double advantage for me. I was able to show through one company-sponsored event (1) that I had security connections in the country and (2) that I was an influential member of the local security community. A colleague from a major oil company managed to secure the presence of senior officers from a neighbouring emirate and it became a lavish occasion with beautiful flower displays, elegant secretaries, interesting talk, a good audience, a sophisticated lunch, and the management—who sponsored the day far beyond what I had expected—made this experience a resounding success that reflected positively on the security department and its manager. The general manager opened the session, the ASIS chapter chair made a speech about ASIS International—giving an international flavor to the day—and I introduced the speaker, who delivered a solid presentation. You may not need to launch such a glamourous event. Sometimes a small note posted on the company's intranet may do. You may simply issue small policies, for example, to sensitize employees to issues such as social engineering, the necessity to protect the company's information, and so on. Try to select a topic that employees find interesting and so benign that nobody will dare challenge it.

The clean desk policy, for example, could simply state that people need to lock their office when they leave the office, clean their desk, not leave their computer unattended, and use the shredder located near the photocopy machine—all things that everyone knows they should do anyway. What matters is that it must be endorsed by the top management to send the right signal to the personnel: *The executive management supports the initiative and there will be others...*

This also means that you need to have relative access to the CEO, not all the time, but when you feel the need, and when you want his support. Do not overuse the privilege. Remember that the CEO deals at a strategic level, and details of the day-to-day running of the business are left to subordinates (people like you and me).

These subordinates must become your allies. It is necessary for you to be able to contact them whenever there is any overlapping issue involving security and their department.

INFLUENCE THROUGH CREDIBILITY

At the end of the day, you will be listened to only if you manage to establish your credibility within the leadership of your organization. This is part of strategic planning. There is no reason you should not be able to attain the status of an HSE or HR person of your same rank. To achieve this, you need to work on the two sides of the same coin. You must increase your competence as a security professional (this is what you are doing by reading this book, but more will be needed), and you must also acknowledge that a security manager is also that, a manager! You may not be the best manager in the world, but you can at least try to look the part and behave like one. If you think you are a competent manager, you will inevitably become one, provided you work for it, of course. The qualities you must show, and that will make all the difference in the eyes of your hierarchy, are the following:

Leadership
You must appear as a leader, not like an old security guard in a striped suit. In many countries where I worked, this is how a security manager is perceived. An ex-police or ex-military person looking to complement an insufficient pension, or a guard who went through the ranks and has little to offer in terms of management skills. Position yourself as someone with ideas, and someone with a will to put these ideas into practice. Show leadership qualities, and encourage such qualities in your subordinates, up to a point.

Consult and innovate, listen to your peers, but also your superiors and your workforce; get ideas, introduce metrics, learn about crime prevention through environmental design (CPTED), be proactive, qualify as a Certified Protection Professional (CPP) or a Physical Security Professional (PSP) through ASIS International, and become a pillar of your ASIS or Overseas Security Advisory Council (OSAC) local chapter. Take responsibilities in the security world. There will be dividends! At the end of the day, it is all about taking responsibility and doing things that need courage. Acting as a leader will make a leader of you and it will be noticed.

Behave as an Executive
This is easier said than done. It may be that your role does not allow you to sit with the big guys. If this is the case, there is not much you can do about it. I knew of a brilliant security manager (a Canadian national) who reported to the facilities manager of his company. Consequently, he was only a head and reported to a manager. He was perfectly qualified to be a manager, he was a CPP, had done a full career in the Canadian mounted police, but the position he applied for was at that level, and since the money was acceptable, he accepted it. This generated issues, though. Every security request was to be vetted first by a manager who was not a security person, and who probably felt threatened by the enthusiasm and dynamism of his subordinate. Worse for his status, he had almost no access to the other managers, and as such could not really work on his appearance as an executive. This man was a great security professional and I admired him very much. But he was in a situation that was not helping him in terms of advancement. How could he be perceived as an executive when reporting to a manager? His status confirmed the image still deeply rooted in many organizations that the head of security is what Sennewald called *the company policeman* (Sennewald 2003: 44). If this is your case, the way out of it is through education. Attend upper and middle management development programs that are designed to enhance a wide range of managerial skills. Such attendance puts the security manager into one-to-one contact with company executives, which can result in meaningful relationships throughout the organization (Sennewald 2003: 44). Take self-development courses and public-speaking courses, volunteer for any course you are offered, and be ready to pay for those

that will promote your career and you as a person. Get involved in the local chapter of ASIS, prepare for the CPP or PSP certifications, take responsibilities in the chapter, join the chapter committees, make yourself known, and become a lynchpin. Improve both your security and your management skills. And meet people: in conferences, in talks, in clubs. To exist and make yourself a name, you must belong! Yet, if your position is poorly located in the chain of command, chances are that you will stay stuck in this subaltern position for longer than you need. My advice is simple: Start looking for another job. Credibility will come at that price. A position that does not provide any window for an opportunity of promotion must be abandoned sooner rather than later. I recently took too long to realize that the job I was doing could not evolve in any way. It took me some time to get out of this tight corner, but I have just succeeded. I have taken up a new position for a little bit less money, but with prospects for evolution. And here lies the secret for you. You must be able to project yourself into a better future and to do so you must behave like an executive, dress like an executive, and think like one.

Look the Part
Your comportment, grooming, and attire should be equivalent to that of the other executives of the company. I once read somewhere that you should adopt the dress code of the level just above yours, to show management that you are ready to move to the next position, but not try to look like the chairman, whose immediate subordinates may resent you and see your behavior as threatening. This advice makes very much sense, and as usual, common sense will lead you to the correct level of elegance. Do not overdo it! But look the part for two reasons: because getting dressed like a business person makes you think like a business person. A suit and a tie provide you with the business armor to fight your way in the day-to-day activities of your organization. Battle dress does not make a soldier, but it contributes… Second, it shows that you are ready to move to the next echelon. Don't be too flamboyant, though, as it will appear pretentious. Be smart and elegant, and wear the right shoes—and polished, please!

Be Visible, Seek Exposure
Always make yourself available for presentations, inside and outside of the company. Join global security associations such

as ASIS International (worldwide), the Security Institute (UK), the IPSA (USA), or any other association of security or related occupation professionals. If you operate abroad, get involved with OSAC, the Overseas Advisory Council, even if you are not American—they accept security professionals irrespective of the color of their passports—join their chapters, volunteer, network, make friends, and take responsibility. People love being members of committees but when it comes to doing real work, wills waver. You can show your mettle there and somehow become a driving element of your chapter.

Think about public speaking. This is the easiest way to get professional exposure. I know that many people fear the idea of speaking in front of audiences more than anything else, except sickness and death. Yet, this is the quickest way to establish yourself as a specialist in any field. In spite of what you might think, public speakers are not hardened professionals with massive experience and thousands of stories to tell. Most of them are regular security practitioners, who, most of us, choose to deliver a talk about a topic they like, and often, because they were asked to. Think about it. See yourself listed in regional and even international events as speakers. Imagine the difference it would make about the way people—and particularly the management of your organization—will perceive you. You will have to ask permission to go and speak abroad, often the green light is given at the highest echelon. Suddenly it puts you on the map, even if you are not yet the greatest speaker the world has seen—or heard!

The only thing that makes you more visible than public speaking is writing a book. And this demands much more work. If you want to give it a try, start by proposing a topic to your ASIS chapter, or propose a topic at a regional conference. Conference organizers need speakers to attract customers. Choose a topic you feel comfortable with. Follow the advice of professional speakers or of those who made them. Books by Dale Carnegie, although decades old, are as valid today as they were 60 or 70 years ago. People always liked listening to others who have the courage to address them. You will find the books I found most useful in this chapter's bibliography. Public speaking may be what you need, and do not get too worried if you don't really feel up to the task when you begin. The secret of public speaking is about experience and finding your style.

And to get experience you must speak as much as you can. The more you talk, the less boring you become (or so I hope…). Regarding your style, it is very simple. You must be yourself. Every time my children go to auditions or job interviews, I repeat the same thing that must irritate them tremendously. I just tell them: be yourself. I honestly don't know if it made a difference, but I think that if you try to be someone else than yourself, you are doomed to fail.

Internally, you must also be visible. To achieve this, start by making yourself available for all security personnel in your organization; be an approachable manager, not only in words—"My door is always open"—but in reality. It will impact the motivation of the guards and the creation of loyalty, and it will in turn provide sources of information—as a security manager you will need to have an intelligence network—and it will create a wealthy climate within the security department and the organization (Sennewald 2003: 45). Show windows of opportunity to your workforce. All security officers and supervisors want more training, more skills, more respect, always. Find ways to open doors for them to keep them motivated. Organize internal trainings. Training does not need to be expensive, but it must be acknowledged and registered in the personnel files. They also have a career.

Make yourself available for other managers as well. Increase your corporate visibility. This is a bit more complicated because it is difficult to create conditions where you will be visible at a corporate level. I was never very good at that but I knew a security manager in a gas company in the Gulf Cooperation Council (GCC), who was really, really good at it. How did he do that? Through the training of local people. He organized training sessions, courses, for young locals and used the taste of Arabs for lavish events by making the certificate presentation a corporate, and even sometimes a national, event by having the press invited, showing his interest and concerns for the transfer of skills from Westerners to locals. It was a very clever operation, because it promoted young talent, and made him most visible at the corporate level. He was often in the newspaper, which cannot really hurt! Of course, if you are operating in a European or North American context, this will not apply, but this idea may inspire you. The concept is to ensure your own promotion by showing your interest in a topic, displaying generosity and apparent self-effacement while gaining positive exposure…Clever and effective.

Become an Advisor

You must become an in-house consultant to your company. A few years ago, I became the first security director of an organization. Before I joined, security tasks were entrusted to the HR manager, a very experienced and effective man. For him, the main job of the security director was to find a consultant to do the job for him. This is a belief about security that I have found quite common in corporate circles. The moment you start wearing a tie, your competences seem to shift toward selecting other people to do the (your) job. I never really espoused this concept and preferred to do the job myself or give it to my own people, that I could guide and monitor. There are reasons for doing security jobs in-house. First, by doing the job, you keep yourself sharp and competent, as it is very easy in the security business to lose that edge. Unless you have to—a risk assessment, for example, should be performed by an external consultant for obvious impartiality reasons—keep the work in-house. It is also good to propose your services to other managers when you feel there is a need. Use your knowledge to become a trusted advisor to the leadership within the company. This will happen only if you have followed my advice to improve your education, skills, and visibility. This is an ongoing process with no end. But this is the right path to exposure and your passport toward an executive management position and more fulfilling tasks in your existing organization or elsewhere.

Be a Trainer

This is an important element of leadership and it contributes to your visibility. Training is one way to make you appear "in charge." Training is what security officers and personnel crave, and usually there is very little budget to train the guard force. If you are like most security managers, with little or no budget, the solution is simple: Create in-house training. Use your resources to create a training program for security personnel. Kane (2000) has written an authoritative and at the same time practical book on the topic and every security manager should have their own copy on their desk. It opens avenues for organizing meaningful training sessions and help maintain the high spirit of the guard force. It will help you create your own courses, complete with several levels of competence worth giving in-house certificates. Take this in-house training into account when promoting guards and since budgets are always scarce, keep the external training opportunities for the best students within your force. Also think about Internet training. I took very interesting courses with the S2 institute and their distance-learning courses are excellent (and no, they do not give me any commission on sales!). While I was writing this chapter I had a quick look at their website which is worth a visit. Without stealing content, you can get inspiration from their work and build PowerPoints to address specific security issues you may have on site. If you manage to make security training interesting, you will increase loyalty and foster a sense of pride often lacking in security personnel.

Training of your staff is, of course, crucial, but also think about security awareness for the employees. Organize talks (early morning, with coffee, croissants, and jam) about social engineering, espionage, and clear desk policies. Make them short, with a good PowerPoint presentation (15 slides max), and keep 10 minutes to answer questions. If you find the right tone, these little briefings will become very popular and will reflect positively on security in general and on you in particular.

Be a Strategic Planner

Last but not least, since this is a book about strategy, you must be a goal setter and a strategic planner.

Goal setter for yourself, for your men and women, and for your department. At each level of responsibility, you must establish a program that takes into account the objectives of the organization, along with the legitimate aspirations of the people who compose your workforce and your personal career. These three levels should not be separated. The idea that you should sacrifice your own objectives to the greater good of the company (whatever that means) is badly reminiscent of my army days. I did not believe in it then, and I do not believe in it now. You must look after yourself properly to look after the others well. This is not selfishness but global planning. You lead the way and for this you must be a self-fulfilled person. You must feel no frustration about your job and your tasks if you want to do them well, and get adherence from your subordinates. In short, you must look ahead for you and your team and do it with a vision (Figure 2.1).

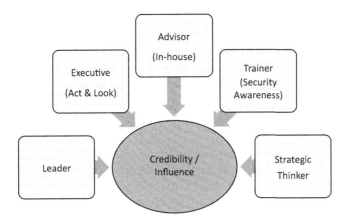

Figure 2.1 Roles that increase the security manager credibility and influence.

SUMMARY

A good security program is only as good as its implementation. To make sure it is implemented, it is crucial for the organization's CEO to support the program. For this to happen, you need to understand management's expectations of security department performance and clearly show that you bring security solutions to existing problems. In other words, your security program will be supported as long as it is reasonable (financially mainly, but also culturally) and seems to solve security issues. Best practice, good-to-have devices, and fancy features have little chance of seducing management because they *cost* money and do not *solve* problems.

Management expects you to be a leader, an executive, and a strategic planner, but also someone with the financial interests of the company at heart. You must never appear as the man who wants to buy gadgets to make security look good. But you can make security look necessary, creative, and effective by applying the sum of the principles and hints given in this chapter. By applying if not all of them at least most of them, you will slowly but surely attract the confidence of your hierarchy and best serve your security program and the people that this program comprises.

Management expects you to produce the best security program at the minimum cost. Always keep the financial costs in mind, particularly when discussing physical (technical) security improvement. The cost/benefit ratio is at the core of all business thinking and you must adopt that way of thinking.

Do not do security for the art of it. You must solve existing security issues or problems. If there is no security problem, do not look for security solutions. Focus on issues and the cheapest ways to answer them. By doing so, you will increase your credibility as a manager. You must always have a clear idea of "how much security is enough" for your hierarchy.

MAIN POINTS

- Your management has expectations of what security should be. Your first task is to understand these expectations.
- These expectations are clearly cost related. Do not ever propose grand schemes unless it is a top-management requirement.
- You will be judged on your ability to solve problems, and your solutions must provide benefits to your management.
- When possible, take the problem away from the decision maker.
- Build your credibility by playing the part of an executive, a strategic thinker, and an advisor.
- Make yourself visible. Security people tend to like shadows. You must make yourself conspicuous!

REFERENCES

Adair, J. (2009) *The Art of Creative Thinking: How to be Innovative and Develop Great Ideas*. Kogan Page: London, UK.

Dalton, D. (2003) *Rethinking Corporate Security in the Post 9/11 Era: Issues and Strategies for Today's Global Business Community*. BH Elsevier: Boston, MA.

Kane, P. (2000) *Practical Security Training*. Butterworth Heinemann: Boston, MA.

Kovacich, G. L. & Halibozek, E. P. (2003) *The Manager's Handbook for Corporate Security: Establishing and Managing a Successful Assets Protection Program*. BH Elsevier: Burlington, NJ.

Sennewald, C. A. (2003) *Effective Security Management*, 4th ed. BH Elsevier: Amsterdam, the Netherlands.

3

Building and Implementing the Security Program

INTRODUCTION

The previous chapter focused on the possible ways to present your security program to executive management and gain their support, as well as how to make you a more visible, more "strategic" person by enhancing your credibility through leadership, education, and professional commitment.

In this chapter, we will continue applying strategic thinking to the way you need to implement your security program throughout the organization.

In this chapter, I am going to focus on the management of change, because upgrading security in an organization is first and foremost about implementing changes, and managing how employees and management react to them. A strategic approach is needed to manage all the changes that your actions will create, and this is what we are going to focus on right now. The idea is not to provide the reader with the perfect security master plan, but to list the activities needed to create such plan and provide a reasonable framework for implementation.

A SECURITY MASTER PLAN TO DO WHAT?

Giles defines a security master plan as:

> A security master plan is a document that delineates the organization's security philosophies, strategies, goals, programs and processes. It is used to guide the organization's development and direction in these areas in a manner that is consistent with the company's overall business plan. It also provides a detailed outline of the risks and the mitigation plans for them in a way that creates a five-year business plan. (Giles 2009: xix)

This definition is enough to show that the security master plan should be the ultimate target of the security executive in a corporate position. As a matter of fact, I believe that there should be a logical link from the vision and mission statement of the organization, its business plan, down to the procedures and processes. This would look rather like this (Figure 3.1):

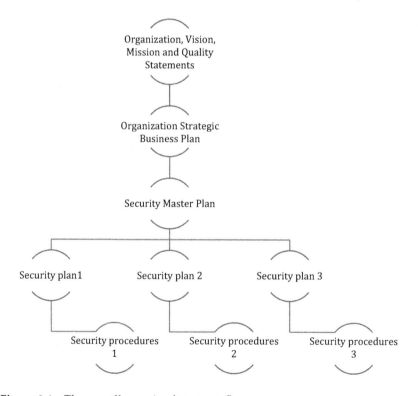

Figure 3.1 The overall security document flow.

As the above figure suggests, the security master plan provides the answers to the philosophy, the strategies, and the limits of the security organization as defined in the business plan. As such it reflects the security spirit of the organization. It could be defined as *the security that we want*. The security plan that stems from this security master plan would be the *how we intend to organize security in order to satisfy the policies, that is, what is our plan to succeed?* The principles of the SMP need to be implemented at all facilities, subsidiaries, and affiliates, but they must be adapted to each particular environment. This is why each entity needs a specific security plan. The procedures that follow are the applications to every aspect of life in the workplace that each and every site will have to implement. While there would be a corporate security master plan, each site, be it headquarters, industrial site, mine, overseas subsidiaries, and so on, would have to develop its specific security plan, served by an appropriate set of procedures.

There is some logic in this, although it is not always easy to articulate and to differentiate.

CONTENTS OF THE SECURITY MASTER PLAN

The new security master plan that you and your team will devise shall consist of the full gamut of policies, procedures, and recommendations to improve the current security posture of the organization. However, I think that corporate security should mainly be involved in the policy portion of the security master plan since these are the policies that will determine the contents of the different security plans of sites and subsidiaries. Although the security master plan will include the whole set of documents for the entire organization, the role of the security director and team is to provide the framework that security managers will use to write their security plan or program.

The master plan you have prepared has been endorsed by the executive management with recommendations to downsize some of your demands, create as little turmoil as possible with the personnel, and try to implement the changes adopting a relatively low profile.

These recommendations are wise suggestions and you will do well to follow them.

A lot has been written on how to manage change within a corporation. As this chapter is about strategic thinking applied to corporate security, we are going to use this wealth of knowledge and try to adapt it to our specific needs. We are going to understand what forces you will be dealing with and how you will use them to reach your goals.

Before we start discussing the "philosophical" side of the SMP, we need to reflect on what I believe should precede the plan.

The security master plan is a topic that has been approached with much success by Kovacich and Halibozek (2003) and more recently by Giles (2009).

To start with, it is important to emphasize that the demand for the security master plan must emanate from the top. It will be extremely difficult for you, if you are not supported, to impose a SMP if your management does not feel the need for such massive document. Bear in mind that it is a corporate document, and therefore echoes the overall global security policy of the organization. Depending on how your organization is structured and your role/position in the organigram, you may not be asked to perform such massive work. Yet, I believe that the SMP should be the starting point that will establish your competence and have you perceived as adding value.

Several points need to be considered when starting the draft of the security master plan. First, it must be produced by the highest authority in security. If there is a VP of security, the SMP must be seen as emanating from him, even if you write the stuff. Authority, when it comes to security, is everything. Why this need for authority? The main reason is that the authority issuing the document should not be challenged. This is particularly important in the case of big companies with many subsidiaries. I have seen many cases of field entities changing, modifying, and creating new policies and procedures on their own authority, without referring to corporate security, sometimes changing the spirit of the program—and this cannot be tolerated. The corporate security manager—who is the originator of the security master plan—is often a person based in the headquarters (HQ), with no real authority over subsidiaries, or the guard force itself, and often has no access to them. Her authority will not be challenged when an authority at the VP or C-level issues the master plan.

Foreword to Administrative Security: What It Really Entails

Administrative security represents the bulk of the security master plan and deals essentially with policies, plans and procedures.

My feeling is that the SMP should be prepared by the security director at HQ and the security plans should be drafted by the highest security personnel in each facility. This is not always possible, particularly when there are many sites and not enough people to man them. In that case, the security director will have to write the plans, and of course, align those plans with the master plan. I was blessed a decade ago with having in my department very strong unit security managers, guys who could have easily played my role, and it was not always simple to synchronize our documents, for a myriad of reasons. But we managed quite well to do so and the workload appeared equitably dispatched between HQ and operational sites. I have also witnessed operations where the security department comprise mainly security supervisors and shift leaders who do not have the capacity to draft procedures. Although it is an important part of security, I find it very strange that there are no training courses on the redaction of policies and procedures. I think writing a post-order is probably as important as watching monitors in a CCTV control room. The fact perhaps comes from the fact that specialized consultants are often brought in to write the documents. Yet, I think procedure writing should be part of the skills necessary to ensure promotion in a security structure.

When the security director is responsible for drafting the plans of the units, subsidiaries, or sites, he will have to visit these sites and meet the people there, and this is all for the best. It shows that you care about these people who often feel isolated and neglected. It will also bring your attention toward issues that you might have missed in your office. This period of reconnaissance is definitely the most exciting period for the newly appointed director! It must clearly be done thoroughly while at the same time keeping an eye on the pulse at headquarters. Remember? You have been hired because there was a security issue in the company, and the management is expecting to see results quick. It is therefore crucial to balance your time between acquiring a good knowledge of the organization's components, people, and culture, while thinking about a few things that could make a difference and buy you time to do your work in-depth. There is a difficult balance there but remember that work which is not seen cannot be not acknowledged.

Drafting this security master plan is, by far, the most important area of corporate security, firstly because "plan, policies and procedures and processes bring order to an otherwise chaotic environment" (Kovacich 2003: 163). For Fay (1999: 1) a policy is a high-level overall statement of the general goals of an organization.

I would like to come back briefly to what differentiates plans, policies and procedures, and processes and in which order they could be conceived. While Kovacich and Halibozek consider their order of importance as plan, policies, and procedures, the plan being first to reflect the commitments issued from the other strategic plans (business plan, tactical business plan, and annual business plan) I am uncomfortable with this approach and suggest that policies should come first.

Why? because the security policies of the organization seem to me driving forces behind the security program. I agree that the plan cannot exist in a vacuum, but the plan needs to be based on some sort of security principles the organization subscribes to. These principles to me should be leading the security plan which will in turn drive the procedures, and ultimately the processes.

A Few Definitions

What is a policy? From the Free Dictionary, a policy is "a plan, or course of action, as of a government, political party, or business, intended to influence and determine decisions, actions and other matters."

From the Business Dictionary, policies are defined as:

> A set of policies are principles, rules and guidelines formulated and adopted by an organization to reach its long-term goals and typically published in a booklet or other form that is widely accessible. Policies and procedures are designed to influence and determine all major decisions and actions, and all activities take place within the boundaries set by them. Procedures are the specific methods employed to express policies in action in day-to-day operations of the organization. Together, policies and procedures ensure that a point of view held by the governing body of an organization is translated into steps that result in an outcome compatible with that view. (http://www.businessdictionary.com/definition/policies-and-procedures.html)

This definition seems to me the most appropriate and provides a good framework on which to establish the security master plan. A plan, according to Fay (1999: 69), is "a detailed formulation of a program of action," while procedures are "a series of steps followed in a regular definite order" (Fay 1999: 135).

I believe that there should be a logical link between every element of the security program and suggest that we should start our master plan, or security program, at the source of the organization's business strategy and begin with studying the vision, mission, and quality statements of the organization that employs us.

Vision, Mission, and Quality Statements

Vision statements are very short pieces of literature, usually from a line to a paragraph long, that define the strategic goals and objectives of the organization in a compact formula. It seems logical to calibrate the security department's vision with the vision of the overall strategic business plan, but it is often difficult to find something that makes sense or does not look empty. A vision could be something like "Building a security program to protect the organization, its employees, and its tangible and intangible assets," or anything in the same vein. You cannot really be wrong by saying this. But it gives the general feeling of what drives you as a security manager. It is therefore necessary.

The *mission statement* defines the purpose of the business or the organization: It can be to build, design, manufacture, produce, and deliver anything, tangible or intangible. The logical, correlated definition for the security department would be to say, "The security department aims to ensure, through an asset protection program, that the organization carries on producing, designing, and manufacturing so and so." Again, you cannot really go astray by stating this or something similar.

Last, the *quality statement* will define what normally "adds value to a corporation's products and service" (Kovacich 2003: 88). For the security department, one could say, "The security department intends to deliver a qualitative approach to all of its activities, documents, and programs. The quality of the service provided by the employees will be continuously monitored in order to serve the organization to the highest level of efficiency and dedication." This is a generic formula that will fit most quality statements for a security department. To these three items, one could add a *policy review statement* stipulating that the security program shall be reviewed every 2, 3, or 4 years.

This document should be the first document to be signed by the top management to show their commitment to the security program and it should appear as the first page of the security master plan.

Policies

Policies fall under administrative security, and as stated are the policies, procedures, and processes that will regulate the security life of the organization.

In his very good book, Fay (1999: 3–67) suggests the following types of policies help clarify what policies can be and what role they play in providing the framework for the security of the organization:

- Affirmative action
- Business ethics
- Conflict of interest
- Deadly force
- Drug and alcohol abuse
- Equal employment opportunity
- Equal employment opportunities for Vietnam-era veterans with disabilities and special veterans with disabilities
- Firearms
- General business
- Harassment
- Health, safety, and environment
- Information security
- Internet
- Investigations
- Political contributions
- Protection of assets
- Physical security
- Security related to sexual harassment
- Smoking
- Special project security
- Travel and entertainment
- Workplace violence

As can be seen by their titles, most of these policies regulate a number of behaviors and establish some clear limits on what is acceptable and what is not. The policies are the rules established by management to work as an employee in the company; they sum up the rights and responsibilities of the workforce. If I were to comment on this list, I would say that a few policies could be added, particularly in a company deployed abroad. Two come to mind:

- A security awareness policy to sensitize the employees, and perhaps the families, to the risk they are facing; not systematically physical risks, but simple risks such as social engineering, for example, which is often overlooked in organizations.

- A VIP security policy to establish the principle of executive protection in the company: the level to qualify, the type of protection,
  the circumstances where it should be used, etc.

Keep in mind that *a* policy is a statement.

One example: Regarding access control, the policy will discuss *who*
should be controlled, *how*, *when*, and by *whom*. It will also stipulate which
areas will be more specifically monitored, because of their operational or
symbolic importance, and the reasons behind this surveillance will somehow determine the badging policy.

The way you present these policies is relatively based on your own
personal experience and preferences and those of the organization for
which you work since there is no magic formula for them. It is up to you,
really, to adopt a standard for your documentation and as long as you can
say everything you want to say in a policy, and that all policies follow the
same pattern, it is acceptable. The template I mostly use when writing
policies for customers is as follows:

A *purpose* in which I define the purpose of the document.
A *scope* in which the limits of the document are explained as well
  guidance for their implementation given.
A list of *definitions* and *acronyms*
Responsibilities: This is obviously a very important paragraph, where
  responsibilities regarding the policy are detailed from the CEO
  level down to the employees' level.

This is usually followed by a *validity* period and a very important *methodology* section.

Methodology is where the policy is analyzed and summarized, and its
step-by-step implementation is detailed. This is normally the substance of
the policy.

Then may come the *policy review* that gives a time limitation on the
validity of the policy. Finally comes the *approval,* which traditionally
includes the signatures of the CEO and the highest security authority in
the organization (CSO or VP of security), followed by appendices, maps,
charts, or processes.

Security Plans

The security plan can be defined as the program of action that each
business unit will develop to ensure the security of their assets.

Fay lists a number of plans, or parts thereof, that could be developed. I cite a few of them:

- Access control
- Bomb threat
- Building emergency
- Business continuity
- Civil disturbances
- Country evacuation
- Extortion
- Fire emergency
- Kidnapping
- Physical security
- Security awareness
- Severe weather

Security practitioners may sometimes find it difficult to differentiate between policies and procedures. Here is a simple trick. If you can add the word *plan* to the topic you want to deal with and that sounds familiar and acceptable, then you can consider it to be a plan. One example: The country evacuation is traditionally a plan; the policy would be that there should be an evacuation plan for expatriates deployed abroad under specific circumstances (remember that a policy is a statement). How we intend to get our people out is the plan.

The same works for security awareness. The policy would be that all employees will receive security awareness training as part of their training and skills improvement. (This is a statement.) The security awareness plan details how the security awareness sessions will be organized and for whom.

Often, you will find in the introduction to the plan a reminder of the organization's policy on the topic. The plan that follows outlines the list of actions to be taken to face the threat or issue.

Security Procedures

Here again, confusion exists between several words: *procedures, processes, post-orders.*

A procedure is a series of steps followed in a regular, definite order.

A process is a series of actions or steps taken in order to achieve a particular end.

In other words, *process* and *procedure* are synonyms. I prefer to use the word *procedure* because it reminds me of standard operating procedures, something used intensively in health and safety fields. A standard operating procedure, or SOP, is a set of step-by-step instructions compiled by an organization to help their employees carry out complex routine operations. It has a flavor of discipline that I like. But put simply, they are procedures that all and sundry must apply to ensure the efficiency of the operation.

Post-orders, if they aim at efficiency, are something different. They are documents that clearly outline duties, responsibilities, and expectations of security officers during their shift. In this they are comparable to procedures. But what makes post-orders particular is that they apply to any security officer that fulfils the role at that post. They are procedures linked to a post. What is a post? It can be one of the positions at the main gate—monitoring CCTV, checking badges, surveillance of incoming vehicles. These are three different posts at the same location. It can be monitoring screens in the security control room; it can be patrolling the site, by car and on foot. Each of these tasks requires a security officer, and post-orders are written to tell the security officers what they have to do. Post-orders belong to the post and each security office must comply with what the post-order say. What makes the post-order confusing is that some of them are written like procedures, which is normal since they tell the officer what steps he should take when faced with a number of different situations. Suffice it to remember that post-orders are documents that are located in a place—the post—often in a folder or displayed on the wall, and that the purpose of post-orders is that they are to be applied by the security office on duty.

Fay (1999) provides a list of 50 procedures that all should find their place in a facility's security plan and that I shall not enumerate. They cover issues as different as bomb threats, background checks, employee access control, and executive protection. I found this book very useful when I wrote my first security plan in the early 2000s and I recommend it warmly. You will probably drop some policies or procedures that do not concern you, and add some, but the template provided will help you deliver a uniform plan that is both comprehensive and applicable.

The Security Program

You have written, discussed, controlled, finalized, and submitted the whole security plan to your management, and it has been approved, without changes (or with minor changes). This is an immense achievement that should make you proud. Whatever happens now to your security master plan, you have produced a document, which can, in the great lines, serve as a model for further master plans.

The life of a security practitioner is full of documents that are remodeled and adapted to new companies operating differently in other circumstances but which all need security master plans based on comparable security principles. This work you produce will not be valid forever, times and threats change, but should you change jobs, or rather when you change jobs, you will have a framework to start from. Of course, I hear you mention the issue of confidentiality and the fact that you cannot keep a security plan belonging to an organization on your computer once you have delivered the product. Absolutely right. This is why you must anonymize it by erasing the name, the location, and any other data related to business operations and deliverables. This can be done without any breach of confidentiality. I was subcontracted once to deliver an evacuation plan for an organization in East Asia, and the consultancy that contracted with me provided me with a template of an evacuation plan that had already been used in several other countries for different customers. It was impossible, from this template, to relate it to any existing company, past or present. But of course, this template saved a lot of my time and was important for the consultancy. Their deliverables needed to be recognizable, and the contents had to be comparable. In fact, it is impossible not to work from a template in such circumstances. You must do the same and save a "clean" copy for reference in your files. You should do this for all the specific types of documents, emergency plans, business continuity plans, business impact analyses—if you also work in business continuity, plans, crisis plans, and policy plans and procedures—and this personal library will help you tremendously in your work as a consultant or as a security executive.

All this is to say that having completed this security master plan not only is your first major action as a security director, it also provides templates, and more importantly, it instills you with self-confidence.

FROM SECURITY MASTER PLAN
TO SECURITY PROGRAM

Now your task as a strategist is the logical implementation of this huge plan through a time-bound schedule and this is really the difficult part of the task. By experience, I can already tell you that it will not go smoothly. What lies ahead of you are closed faces, bad-mouthing, unpleasant looks,

Figure 3.2 The logical unfolding of security.

and so on. You will have to fight on several fronts, at different levels, and this will last until the last of your changes has been implemented. People do not like change, because they feel threatened in their daily routine (Figure 3.2).

Before you begin preparing your implementation sequences, prioritizing what needs to be done yesterday and what can wait a bit, you need to be aware that from now on, you will have to find the right tone and attitude to implement a security program that has been acknowledged by the C-suite but that will be passively—and sometime overtly—resisted by the workforce. Yet, if the best security master plan is not implemented, you will have the feeling of having failed. As a strategist, this is something you do not even want to envisage. To put all the chances on your side, you need first to understand what change entails, and to anticipate the capability of inertia of the workforce in the organization and plan for success.

UNDERSTANDING CHANGE

There are several types of changes that can apply to security as a business unit of the organization. Usually, in security, change is the result of a decision taken at the highest level, since only executive management can impose changes of such nature. Security is a regalian prerogative and as such, policies, plans, and procedures should be obeyed by the workforce.

The reasons behind changes can be numerous. It can be that the company is new and that a security master plan has just been prepared—this is the case that we are discussing right now. It can be as a result of a poor response to a security incident, or it can be imposed after a merger between companies where one of the partners has more stringent standards or security requirements.

But whatever the case, a change in security always comes from the top, and as such, gives you some kind of undeniable authority in its implementation phase.

Of course, you will be perceived by the workforce as the man behind the program, while you are the man that implements the decisions of the CEO, or the board, and this give you a mix of authority and flexibility about the way you will implement this program. Pending on circumstances or who is facing you, you may want to play the card of the regular guy who is just doing his job, but you must be cautious with this kind of attitude, even if sometimes it looks like easier path when facing unhappy employees. Somehow you have been chosen to implement security measures that everybody knows will be unpopular and when challenged you must stand your ground. This is what is expected from you. This does not mean that a bit of diplomacy will not work miracles. But you must take responsibility for the content of the program and you must always give the feeling that security—like safety, by the way—is not something negotiable.

PLANNING CHANGE

Coming now to the task at hand, you will have to plan the coming changes very carefully. You must first consider what you think is not acceptable in the current security department. Since you took office as the security director, you have been a keen (and often silent) observer of what happens in the department and you have formed a good picture of where your organization stands in terms of security. With this picture in mind, and with the objectives that you received from the CEO, you have established a security master plan that describes where you want to take the security department in the near-to-medium term future (the strategic vision).

Establishing these start and finish points is a first step in identifying where changes are needed (Heller 1998: 16). There are five steps in the process:

1. Your current situation. This is the starting point of the process. Write down as precisely as possible the existing security situation as it is perceived by the security department.
2. Where you want to go. This is your target. Reaching the target within a defined period of time will create situations of change. For now just write down the specific targets that your security department wants to achieve.
3. Quantify the gap; in other words, list precisely what is going to change and how it will affect people. Every time something affects people, it will be resisted. Get ready for it. Write down how

these changes might be resisted. Use your security guard force experience if they are a seasoned lot.
4. Map out the changes that need to occur to reach the target or targets. In other words, list step by step how you will implement the new security plan. It might be a good idea to do some reverse thinking and start from the ideal outcome then see how this perfect outcome was attained.
5. Write these changes down as precisely as possible and use them as a guideline for the department. Your staff must know where you want to go and how you and they will succeed.

From this brainstorming session, you will end up with a lot of changes. These changes are the milestones that will take you to where you want your department to be.

PRIORITIZING CHANGES

You must expect your new security program to create anxiety among employees. There is a danger in overwhelming people with too many changes, too fast. Changes need to be swallowed in measured quantities and success lies with their regular distribution at homeopathic doses. Before you set your priorities a few points to remember:

- Change in one area may affect other areas. Try to anticipate these implications and avoid bad surprises.
- The strategic reasons for change should be widely publicized, either on the intranet, in the organization's newspaper, or on information boards. Communicate!
- Only change that is people based will work in the long term. You must therefore get employees' support.
- Everyone involved in the change should be consulted beforehand. Nothing is worse than having to backtrack, but you may have to if you have misread or misunderstood consequences of the changes you want to implement!
- Planned changes should not be made in one go. Go one step at a time. Monitor reactions and move again with caution.
- Change needs to be categorized into high, medium, and low priorities.

Change in One Area May Affect Other Areas

When you start modifying a security plan, chances are that a change in one area will have consequences in another. Consider this example: If you change the delivery of parcels to the mail office, and if the postal worker is no longer allowed to enter the plant/facility/HQ as she used to do, but should deliver her post at main gate, the following might happen. The DHL delivery person will not be able to enter the plant anymore and might have to double park outside the facility or the headquarters, something which, in urban contexts, can create safety risks. You have substituted a security risk for a safety hazard. This is not good! Another consequence could be that one of the security officers will have to bring the post to the mail office in the building, an action he will do at the detriment of another of his tasks.

Another common issue: If you impose that all vehicles parked inside the parking lot will have to show a vehicle identification sticker, what happens when an employee has to borrow her husband's car, because her car had to be taken in for maintenance? Will she be refused entry? A long list can be made to highlight that new security procedures do have an impact on life at work on several levels. Not only will new security procedures imply changes, but these changes may have a cascading effect and morph into a major headache that brings more trouble than real benefit. Any security measure, when implemented, will irritate your employees one way or another. Examples are countless. The important thing is to try to think very carefully about the specific situation of the facility, envision all the possible consequences each change will bring, and try to foresee how employees will react. If you expect resistance to a specific change because of the cascading consequences that will follow, it may not the right time to push that procedure and a bit of waiting is advised, particularly if the security benefit is not obvious. It's not exactly the butterfly effect but a security procedure is never trivial and always carries discomfort when implemented in the real world.

Determining what is urgent is not easy matter. Your job will be to keep a balanced momentum between all parts of the security program. Some areas will be sources of tension; access control, for example, always is, and parking is always a source of conflict. In short, anything that makes an employee's lifestyle less disorderly will probably be fought, challenged, and disobeyed. You must therefore make sure that executive management will follow you when new changes are implemented and rejected by some. Indeed, you can expect some problems, but these problems must not stop the program. You will learn to fix the problems while the implementation plan moves ahead. This is essential in order to maintain your credibility and the implementation plan momentum. You must therefore select your key result areas carefully and ensure that there will be some kind of logic in your way of implementing change.

The Strategic Reasons for Change Should Be Widely Publicized

One often reads that the four functions of security are, in order, deter, detect, delay, and respond to attacks. Though some add recover to this list, I think that recovering from an attack is only partly the role of security and not one of its main functions. You will also see in some books deny—in the sense deny entry—but to deny entry is really one of the functions (with grant and control) of access control rather than a function of the security program. My assessment of these functions is, of course, only an opinion and you may consider including the recovery function in your approach to the security program, or even find some other function that has not been discovered yet. For now, I will concentrate on the main functions of deter, detect, delay, and respond. These are the four axes of effort you must have in mind when putting your program together. Select changes that apply to each of these functions. Privileging one function to the detriment of others is not the right strategy. Working exclusively on deterrence, in other words, focusing on perimeter and gate security, will seldom get you support and will not enhance your reputation in the company. Yes, deterrence is visible by definition, but it is not always a priority and should not be treated in isolation. If you balance changes harmoniously, among the four or five functions, you will convey the feeling that there is a plan in the way you change things and people are more supportive if they understand what you are doing (this is where awareness sessions and intranet communication have a role to play). An improvement to the overall security will be palpable and will benefit you and your team.

The second important thing is how and according to which timescale you will implement these changes. In other words, and I will come back to this later in this book, you need to select with caution your key result areas (KRAs). As the name indicates, a KRA is an area of business that you consider essential to the success of your department. Some will be of your own volition; others may be imposed on you. But they are like the axes of effort that will guide your program. Once the KRAs are selected, you will have to select the famous KPIs to demonstrate that things are going as planned. People talk a lot about KPIs while often ignoring KRAs.

KRAs do take precedence. And for now, your most important task is to select these KRAs and to prioritise them, with three constraints in mind:

- What does the management expect from you? Why did they hire you and what results do they want to see?
- What do you think are the most important loopholes in the security delivery—those things that you have observed since you arrived and that you benchmarked against best practices and previous assignments?
- Which are the areas that will trigger the most testing response from the workforce? Your reflection must bring these three elements into the new equation and you must think carefully about these points. Whatever your choices in each area, you will have to implement them in a timely manner. I did not say slowly, I said timely. Always go for the least disturbing change first. There will be less resistance and if employees find the change tolerable and relevant, their trust in the security department may increase, giving you more leeway for subsequent bolder moves.

Only Change That Is People-Based Will Work in the Long Term

The changes you have in mind will affect the daily life at work for the employees. This is obvious. It is therefore essential that the people who are at the receiving end of the stick find the punishment bearable. You might find these words harsh? They are not. It is human nature to assess every limitation in relation to one's own freedom—and try to work around it to make one's life as easy as possible. Your changes will not be dealt with differently. People will immediately find a way to circumvent them to avoid changing their behaviors. Countless times I have seen safety doors propped open with bricks or stones to make the access to the outdoor smoking area easier for employees. This is just one of many examples of minor acts of indiscipline that weaken your efforts. What are the consequences of this? People will react to your changes by trying to revert to bad habits, and such behaviors need to be discouraged. Once the bad behaviors are stopped, security must act swiftly while avoiding direct conflict. It is not procedures you need to change, but people's attitude toward security, and I do not believe that this can be attained without a bit of castigation. Like the CPTED technique of replacing broken windows incessantly to avoid building decay—it is called the broken window theory—behaviors that do not go in the direction of better security should be stopped until the new behavior is accepted and in place. Once your workforce has accepted the change, they will often be the best champions of this change. It is a strange occurrence but one that has been observed many times.

Everyone Involved in the Change Should Be Consulted

This is easier said than done. When you plan to change the delivery of big parcels or the distribution of mail, it is quite simple to discuss with the people that are involved. It is recommended because, as previously mentioned, changes have cascading effects that you may not have envisioned, and the people who do the job will immediately foresee these effects (and sharply criticize). So, if you want to avoid embarrassment, and nothing is worse than backtracking on a change being implemented, speak with the people involved in the change. If you want to change the location of the parking lot, it is clear that you will not ask the opinions of the whole workforce. You will have to take the issue to a higher level, because such a change will have a huge impact on the workforce, as well as the relationship between employees, between employees and managers, and ultimately between managers…and you!

In a place where I worked somewhere in the Persian Gulf, the security department suggested that all cars be parked outside the facility. This was in the heyday of roadside bombings in Iraq and there were good reasons to prevent cars from parking near the administration building of the company. The management agreed to the plan, and a long, shaded parking space was built outside the entrance. This initiative met incredible resistance from the manager's echelon of the organization (the one just one layer below the one that had made the decision to keep cars outside). They could not accept the idea of walking two hundred meters while finding this perfectly acceptable for lower employees. Some even suggested having a system of valet parking, where managers would give their keys to employees to park their car and bring the car back to them when they left. I guess you know what happened next. Once the facility was up and running, and the last of the expatriates working in the security department had left the place, the parking was reinstated next to the administration building and the external parking was reserved for visitors only. What message do I want to convey with this anecdote? It is always better to consult when you can, and you must be aware of the pre-eminence of cultural issues in many areas of the world. On top of consulting with the employees and management, start discussing your changes with old hands in the region. They will give you a good idea of what can realistically be done and what can't.

Planned Changes Should Not Be Made in One Go

Changes specialists say that changes should be imposed with moderation and at reasonably distant intervals. Heller tells us that "if you introduce too many initiatives in close succession, staff may suffer from overload. Initiative fatigue reveals itself rapidly in falling performance, high stress levels, low morale and diminishing return on initiatives" (Heller 1998: 21). For changes linked to security I do not think that you may reach such terrible situations of loss of morale and low productivity. Security—apart from security officers—is not even part of the work, it is just something that hangs around outside of an employee's core task, like badging, key control, clean desk policies, smoking areas, parking issues, and new photocopy and shredder rules. Although you—as the ultimate security person in the organization—believe that you are the decisive enabler, your colleagues in other departments tend to doubt that. Do not take for granted that the most educated of them support you. They accept your presence and tolerate your actions, they are friendly with you before and after management meetings, they think you managed to grab a good position where there is not much to do apart from looking after a few guards, but they all think that you really are a pain in the neck. There is not a lonelier job than security director (apart from platoon leader or company commander in the field, but that is another story).

The reason is simple and hard to contradict: Before you arrived, life was less complicated and people were perfectly safe. The fact that no incident preceded your appointment is hard to defeat. Do not try to justify yourself; it is pointless and you will convince no one.

Change Needs Fall into High, Medium, and Low Priorities

From all that was said above, and from your own experience, you know that implementing too many changes at the same time is a recipe for failure. You need to prioritize. Refer to the Key Result Areas in Chapter 4 and think about the necessity of determining your needs and immediate actions, and what could wait a bit.

I suggest that you do not multiply the number of levels of prioritization. Three seems reasonable and I would suggest sticking to the standard recommendation of high, medium, and low priorities. One suggestion would be to consider the impact as the major criterion, but there again, there are opposing philosophies: Some suggest beginning with change that will bring the *biggest* impact. The idea is that with a simple action you immediately and visibly provide a result for management. I understand the point, but I am not too sure about doing a big change first. My natural inclination would be to test changes on things that would not taint you as a horrible person it they were not a resounding success. Try things at the canteen, or in the parking lot. Try a clean desk policy, or any issue on which people, deep down, know that improvement is really needed. It will have the advantage of relaxing your relationship with personnel, creating a feeling of acceptance that will probably be stretched to its limits later when you implement more serious security changes. But this is of course a personal choice, and your choice must reflect your personality.

BREAKING DOWN TASKS

Changing the badging system, implementing a visitor's program with security and safety implementation sessions, and training the receptionist to follow a more security-orientated process with visitors are all minor tasks that can be handled more easily than restructuring the whole access control system in one go. Take each of your main tasks and break them into simple, easy to implement and easy to communicate modest tasks. Take them one by one, according to logic. Get the implementation program for visitors ready before you train the receptionist for it. Have the head of safety help you put together a small pamphlet summarizing safety and security measures on site, and issue the pamphlet to each visitor and contractor when they enter the site. Buy the visitor management system software and master it before implementing it at headquarters level. Make sure that when you start implementing a change, it is working and that it is in its rightful place in the implementation program.

CONSULTING AND INVOLVING EMPLOYEES

Involving people is one of the strategies at your disposal, if you want your implementation program to succeed, and it is a central one. But this could be much more complicated than you anticipated. Nickerson, in his seminal book *Leading Change from the Middle*, provides the correct method to do this. Do not forget that as a security director or manager the onus will be on you to implement this security program that you have really nurtured, you and your team. You probably have a boss, the CSO or VP of security; you do not work in isolation. Before you draw up a plan about consulting fellow employees, I suggest you take a deep breath and apply Nickerson's analytical method. What does it consist of? Nickerson suggests that you make a list of all the project stakeholders. By stakeholders, he means anyone and everyone who might need to contribute to the project or could be affected by it (Nickerson 2014: 29).

When dealing with security in the workplace, one could easily claim that everyone will be affected by the security program. This is true. But for now, let us concentrate on those executives or middle managers who can either help you or make your task complicated. Nickerson suggests a two-pronged approach that you need to consider in your implementation program. You must first split your stakeholders into external and internal groups. As discussed previously, the internal stakeholders are quite easy to identify. They are the people in your organization that will be affected by your project. After line managers and other senior leaders, Nickerson brings our attention to a group that "consists of those who perform financial, accounting, legal, human resources and any other staff or overhead function needed to complete the project" (Nickerson 2014: 31). One tends to forget that your changes will impact many cadres in the organization and that these people may not enjoy their boat being rocked; those that especially come to mind are facilities management and human resources, who are often your competitors when it comes to security. Do not expect unconditional support from people who will have their organization disturbed. As you know, when managers do not support you there is a strong possibility that their employees won't either.

Think about including you own people as stakeholders, those involved in the project and others, because they are. On the outside, the obvious stakeholders are the organization's clients and your service providers. A change in the delivery of bulk mail will need to be discussed with DHL or ARAMEX, or whoever you use as a courier company. Think about the service providers that will be impacted by your security program. The other parties will have to be informed before you implement any decision, because they may have constraints that make your plan inapplicable or complicated to implement.

The second thing Nickerson suggests is to cluster the stakeholders. He warns that:

> The varying nature, size, and attitudes of the relevant internal and external stakeholders can introduce much complexity into leading change, especially when doing so from the middle. (Nickerson 2014: 33)

Figure 3.3 Clustering stakeholders.

There may be others that you do not see as external stakeholders. Far-away subsidiaries, headquarters, and regional offices may be considered external stakeholders if they do not have a direct, daily impact on your action because your action may have a delayed impact on their life. Then Nickerson proposes to cluster stakeholders into four categories as shown in Figure 3.3. They are:

    Superordinates: the individuals and groups above your mid-level management organization, including "your immediate supervisor, [and] his own boss up to the point of the organization where a leader is unlikely to care about the outcome of a project" (Nickerson 2014: 34).

    Subordinates: the individuals and groups that report directly to you as well as suppliers, vendors, contractors, and consultants.

    Customers: consist traditionally of internal and external customers. In security, your customer is both your hierarchy and the workforce. Amazingly you provide to both a service but the former is at the origin of the job and the latter is the end user of your work. This is a weird situation, when you think of it, and a difficult one, since, to succeed, you must satisfy the former without antagonizing the latter.

Complementors/blockers: I find this concept by Nickerson brilliant. I never thought of it when I was a corporate security advisor, but in retrospect, it makes perfect sense! Nickerson defines these complementors/blockers as "these individuals who are needed to forge the new capability but who do not report to you and to whom you do not report either" (Nickerson 2014: 34).

This needs a bid of explanation. Who are these people that you need to win to your cause? How are they different from the people that count? In fact, these are the people that can be compared to you, with middle-management capabilities, but who have the capacity to support your project or to block it, and like you, they do count!

> This category is defined by the approval and support required from legal, financial, human resources, purchasing and other units across the organization. These individuals complement the midlevel leader's activities by providing resources, requisite approval, guidance, and other forms of assistance to help build extraordinary capabilities. (Nickerson 2014: 35)

These people can be your best allies and you must try to establish rapport with them as early you as you can.

In summary, when you are ready to implement one of the program tasks, first look at the people concerned by the change, from management down to shop-floor level (superordinates and subordinates), but also people to your right and your left (customers and complementors/blockers). Questions you should ask yourself are:

- Who will be affected by the change?
- Who are the key people that need to be involved?
- How may people react? (Who may provide enthusiastic support and who will probably fight the change?)
- Will people need new skills and training?

The answers to these questions will help you create an action plan.

MAKING AN ACTION PLAN

The action plan you are going to prepare should not be carved in stone. It will be more like a guideline, as forces beyond your control, such as inertia and resistance, will have an impact on the contents of your plan, its implementation, and the associated timeline.

There is specific software you can use to help you create your action plan, but it is often too complicated to use and a nightmare to modify. You can simply use Microsoft Word or Excel to draft the plan, provided you can list (A) the task, (B) the person responsible for it, and (C) the time scale. Of course, being proficient with project management software is definitely something that I would recommend for a security manager. Being qualified as a Project Management Professional (PMP) or a Prince 2 practitioner would certainly add value to your curriculum vitae (CV), while giving you more confidence in implementing the changes.

ANTICIPATING RESISTANCE TO CHANGE

Change is always resisted, no matter what one may say. But you can anticipate this resistance by preparing yourself to face the critics. Thinking strategically at this point means once again anticipating what should and probably will happen.

Point to remember: "People['s] reactions to change follow usually the following pattern: Passive resistance is followed by active resistance, then passive feelings and eventually acceptance" (Heller 1998: 38). This is a normal and well-known process. Allow time for this process to unfold and be ready to be flexible in the implementation of your plan depending on the nature and magnitude of the reaction. But remember that these reactions are emotional and that *reason only* cannot be an adequate response to emotional resistance. Be ready to discuss content with the critics, but remember to give emotional reassurance. Once your plan is up and running, critics will weaken and then fade.

To limit the resistance to changes, you will have to face your critics with sympathy and understand whether their resistance is fueled by "rational objections, personal fears or emotional distrust of change" (Haller 1998: 52).

The following table indicates how to combat the resistance to change according to the nature of this resistance (Table 3.1).

71

Table 3.1 Dealing with Negative Reactions to Change

Types of Negativity	Actions Recommended
Rational	Explain plan with greater clarity and details
Misunderstanding of details of plan	Project what would happen if the change program were not introduced
Belief that change is unnecessary	Involve everybody in quality-improvement teams to demonstrate effectiveness of managed change
Disbelief in planned change's effectiveness	Institute a bottom-up program for reorganizing systems and processes
Expectation of negative consequences	
Personal	Stress much-improved job prospects for the future of everyone
Fear of job loss	Present plans for improvements which people are likely to find positive and exciting
Anxiety about the future	
Resentment at implied criticisms of performance	Accept management responsibility for past failures
Fear of interference from above	Present a scenario showing the anticipated benefits of the main changes
Emotional	Show with examples why the old ways no longer work
Active and/or passive resistance to change in general	Stage a series of meetings to communicate details of the change agenda
Lack of involvement	Demonstrate that the new policy is not merely a flavor of the month
Apathy toward initiatives	
Shock	Explain the reasons for change, and promise involvement
Mistrust of motives behind changes	Be honest and answer all questions

Source: Table originally published in MANAGING CHANGE by Robert Heller (Dorling Kindersley 1998). Copyright © Dorling Kindersley, 1998.

CONCLUSIONS

Applied strategic thinking is essential to manage change in an organization. It is from your capacity to impose your security program that you will be judged, not on the quality of the program itself. A first-class program that ends up on your shelf because all employees rejected it is pointless and humiliating. Executive management will test your managerial abilities according to your capacity to manage change. So, when you write your security master plan, you should, from the inception, think about the possible objections and guaranteed resistance that the program will face at some stage. A plan for every point of resistance must be devised.

Think strategically about your response, your plan, and how you will involve all those who could jeopardize your initiative. Remember to be flexible; some of the resistance may be based on rational objections and you should listen to these objections, and show that you can accept critics for the benefit of the organization.

SUMMARY

To implement a security program is to implement a series of changes that need to be accepted. In Heller's words: "Change is the single most important element of successful business management today." Understanding, planning, implementing, and consolidating change are essential skills for the security manager. To succeed in monitoring security changes, the changes must be selected with caution and then implemented with flexibility while consulting employees and encouraging their involvement. Resistance to change must be anticipated and an action plan devised to respond to this opposition. Implementation must therefore be well conceived upstream, and the least disturbing changes must be implemented first.

Once trust is established, resistance to more consequential changes will diminish. Always try to involve concerned employees in the implementation of the program.

Anticipate resistance and prepare arguments and a plan B, be flexible, and do not hesitate to postpone a change should you be greeted with overwhelming defiance.

MAIN POINTS

- The security master plan should be the first major task of your new assignment, but it should be built while immediate actions and urgent decisions are being taken. Some actions must be immediately visible!
- Vision, mission, and quality statements should precede the SMP and must be approved early by the management, not as an afterthought.

- The implementation of a new security program will be met with resistance, and part of the program is to anticipate this resistance.
- Advertise the changes you intend to make in an informative and friendly way (intranet, company newsletter, etc.).
- Adopt a progressive approach to change from the least controversial to the most difficult to implement.
- Make your security team agents of change.
- Consult and involve as many people as you can in your program.
- Be flexible, attentive, and patient, but keep your main goal in mind: improving the security posture of the organization.

REFERENCES

Fay, J. J. (1999) *Model Security: Policies, Plans and Procedures.* Butterworth-Heinemann: Boston, MA.

Giles, T. D. (2009) *How to Develop and Implement a Security Master Plan.* CRC Press: Boca Raton, FL.

Heller, R. (1998) *Managing Change.* DK Essential Managers: London.

Kovacich G. L. and Halibozek, E. P. (2003) *The Manager's Handbook for Corporate Security: Establishing and Managing a Successful Assets Protection Program.* Butterworth-Heinemann. Amsterdam, the Netherlands.

Nickerson, J. (2014) *Leading Change from the Middle: A Practical Guide to Building Extraordinary Capabilities.* Brookings Institution Press: Washington, DC.

4

Measuring the Security Program

INTRODUCTION

In this fourth chapter, I assume that the implementation of the security program is now well on track and progressing. I also assume that you must now start to think about demonstrating to the executive suite that what you are doing is what they hired you to do. If and when it is not exactly in line, you need to show that you made reasonable and business savvy choices, and that these choices improve the organization's security posture. Simple, is it not? Managers are not security professionals, they can seldom see the greater picture, and a bit of explaining cannot hurt!

Strategic thinking is also crucial to this difficult phase. Always bear in mind that thinking strategically means implementing things in the present to serve the goals of the future. In this chapter, we are going to consider two essential issues in security management. First, we will reflect on how to *consolidate* your security program, and second, how to *measure its effectiveness*.

CONSOLIDATING CHANGE

We left your program where customers—mainly internal—had given up fighting a rear-guard action and decided to accept and endorse the security program after probably a few adjustments from your side. This, in itself, is an achievement you can be proud of. However, do not claim victory too soon. This acceptance from the workforce is conditional and should never be taken for granted. It is up to you to show that you were right to force these changes into the employees' life. Be aware that just because people do not fight the new security procedures anymore does not mean that they think they are valid. You do not need to convince them but you need to gain their trust and the process might prove taxing.

To achieve this, you need to demonstrate, upstream and downstream, that you were right. I do not think there is any other way to make your point than using figures. Nothing is more convincing, at least to the management.

Now is the time to measure the performance of your program. To do so requires some implementation guidelines, perhaps to acquire some new skills.

MEASUREMENTS

Measurements of security performance are used "to show the relevance of the security function to the corporation" (Cole 2003: 101). This is a fine definition provided one understands what is meant by measuring security performance. We will see later in this chapter that the choice of security metrics is crucial to your image, your credibility, and therefore your position as a manager.

There are basically two types of measurements that you can use, and they are usually called hard and soft. As you can guess, hard measurements are things/actions/events that can be counted and recognize as relevant. This is the area of traditional physical security and something that is understandable by all and sundry. Examples are the cost of man-guarding measured against the number of visitors, the number of trucks controlled at the industrial gate, the number of deliveries checked by the guard force, the number of offices opened because of forgotten keys, the number of badges delivered to visitors and contractors, and so on. These are usually the numbers that the security department puts forward to demonstrate their relevance and show that "security is doing something" and provides value for the money spent on it. I do not know if you will agree with me, but my impression is that this kind of metric is not convincing anyone up there. I know that health and safety people have become masters of this kind of measurement and that they are particularly fond of graphics, but I find them a bit puerile, sometimes to the point of embarrassment. The reason is not the use of pies or of colors, but because often they are poorly chosen. I remember reading at organizations I audited security metrics such as *number of entries at gate 2*. There is no doubt that this figure is a measurement, but this is not a metric; it is at best facility management data. The important word in security metrics is *security*. One example: A security metric regarding access control at reception would be the number of people caught tailgating on a specific day or on average during a particular month. This is a security metric. It refers to a figure: the number of people that entered the gate, and another number of people who gained access illegitimately (the word might be a bit strong). The ratio between these two numbers is a metric and a security one. If you say that 250 people passed through reception between 7 a.m. and 9 a.m. on a particular day, and that five people were caught tailgating by security, two really tailgating and three piggybacking, that would be pertinent security information and a valuable statistic. You could assert that tailgating/piggybacking accounts for 2% of morning entries on that date. These data have value because they can be compared over time. Like any metric, it lends itself to statistics and business people talk that language. If some days are more prone to tailgating than others, you might like to understand why. Suggest possible or probable reasons, confirm your hypothesis, and then find a solution to the problem.

Metrics should: (1) provide valuable information and (2) be security related. Non-security data should appear in a report only to provide the capacity of establishing security statistics and not as an end to itself.

A world of caution, though: These measurements are double-edged swords. I have used them in my career and noticed that they had little impact on the usually distrustful opinion of security by the executive management's mind. I give you one real-life example: The security manager of our building HQ had decided to put three guards on duty during the morning rush hour, to face the problems that were currently occurring (badge forgotten, no windscreen sticker, lost keys, boom gate refusing to raise, etc.). In a 30-minute period, most of the employees that were entering the place parked either outside or underground and went through turnstiles, and other entrance areas. It seemed logical to concentrate the bulk of the shift to ensure smooth access to the offices. Both employees and management misunderstood the reason behind this decision, and our security manager was told that the general manager (GM) did not want to see so many security guards when he arrived at work. Their presence gave him the feeling that there were far too many guards in the department and that the guard force could probably be reduced in numbers if three were needed to monitor access in the morning! In his manager's mind, one would have sufficed. This was of course totally unfair, but security had bad press and isn't it all about perception? A strong presence was not perceived as the capacity to solve problems but as too many guards not having anything else to do, deployed conspicuously to appear to do something. Justifying the decision by showing significant hard figures is one way to convince the management that the aggregation of so many people and vehicles within such a short period of time required maximum manpower to ensure a smooth ingress. You may not completely win (in our case, we were asked to hide the guards behind tinted glass in the lobby), because security provides an unpleasant feeling—and no, I did not invent that one! Eventually, the principle that security officers should be deployed at that point in time where the action was, was accepted. The deployment had to be adapted to the environment and local sensitivity; security had to be invisible.

Anyway, coming back to measurements, some are called *soft* measurements. Soft measurements are, in Cole's words, "measurements of performance used for these events that cannot be accurately counted, but can be responsibly projected from an inferred cause-and-effect relationship" (Cole 2003: 103). The example given by Cole is the impact of training on the security force. The number of hours can be measured and counted, but the impact on the performance of the security personnel involved is more difficult to evaluate, although self-esteem, morale, and proficiency are definitely among the benefits of training. Ways to assess these positive outcomes are, in my experience, through observation and survey.

WHAT SHOULD BE MEASURED? AND WHY?

These are the most difficult questions of this chapter, and seasoned professionals could argue on the answers forever. But let us keep thinking strategically. It goes without saying that

> performance measurement should coincide with the mission of the function as well as the corporate goals or vision statement. The key readers want to receive information consistent with the programs they have supported on behalf of the Chief Executive Officer (Cole 2003: 108–109).

The purpose of measurement is to show how the security function contributes to the organization's profitability or efficiency. Easier said than done. But all security practitioners agree that some sort of metric should be used.[1]

Never forget that metrics are indicators of possible unwanted security events in the making. Too many access control violations, cars observed parked around the perimeter at regular time intervals, people standing in observation spotted in front of the headquarters' main entrance, and reported attempts at social engineering are all worrying indicators that reconnaissance may be ongoing and this unpleasant possibility should be dealt with quickly and effectively. These indicators must be recorded and reported, and a surveillance plan, devised by you and your team, with the approval of the executive management, must be quickly put in place. Metrics are therefore an activity report but also an important stimulus for decision making.

CSFs, KRAs, AND KPIs

I am always surprised that customers so often require key performance indicators for the security program without questioning the essence and nature of what a KPI really is. The general public's idea is that KPIs measure performance and therefore if one wants to measure performance, one must use KPIs.

There is nothing wrong with this idea, since the purpose of a KPI is indeed to measure performance. But the KPI is the end result—not the beginning—of a thinking process that starts upstream with a study of the critical success factors and key result areas.

If one is intent on measuring performance, and this is as valid for security as for any other business unit, one should first focus on critical success factors (CSFs). CSFs are elements of a strategy that need to go right in order to ensure the organization's success. Critical success factors are measured according to four criteria: (1) *product attributes*, or the intrinsic value of what you are developing, producing, and selling; (2) *resources*, that is, the quality and number of the resources you have at your disposal to do the task; (3) *competencies*, that is, the capabilities of your employees to serve your strategic objectives; and last (4) your *competitive capabilities*, or how you position yourself among the competition and how you could improve that situation.

Critical success factors are composed of three elements (Figure 4.1):

Core values stem from the vision, mission, and quality statements of the organization. Core competencies are the sum of all the competencies one can rely on in the organization. They are the sum of qualifications, but they are also the ability to work as a group, the motivation of the workforce, and its capability to adapt—all intangible elements of competency that will give an organization an edge over another. Key result areas are of course the areas that matter. Security is a vast concept and your actions

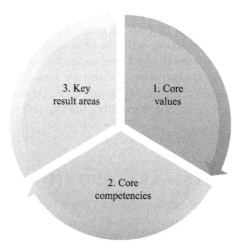

Figure 4.1   The three critical success factors.

will not embrace all of security at the same time. You do not have the budget, you do not have the people, and you probably do not have all the skills needed to do so. The sum of, or rather the relationship between, these three elements is crucial to the success of the security department. As a security executive, you need to carefully monitor this relationship. Balance is needed because you will have to adapt, or increase, core competencies to what you believe should be the key results area. Let us now see how these three elements relate to one another.

CORE VALUES

The core values, developed from the vision, mission, and quality statements, drive competencies. The values we defend and promote in the organization will help define the competencies to be developed in order to perform effectively and reach our strategic goals. Competencies are not only related to the nature of the work. Of course, engineering needs engineering competencies, finance specialists, and administrative competencies. These people are generally recruited on the basis of their qualifications and experience. But there is more to work than just knowing what it is about.

Other core competencies need to be possessed to thrive in the workplace. They are adaptability, capacity to work in a group, dynamism, good interpersonal skills, an extraordinary capacity to be loved or give confidence to clients, public speaking qualities, the ability to always adopt the right or best attitude, and so on. All these elements are part of a person's competency and can rarely be assessed during a job interview. These core competencies once understood are, in turn, the drivers for key result areas, which will prioritize the strategic objectives of the company. Only then will KPIs be created to serve these KRAs.

HOW TO EXTRACT KEY RESULTS AREAS?

I have always found it very challenging to extract critical success factors from traditional organizational strategic goals. There is usually very little reference, if any, to security in these documents, and I remember reading a huge one where the word *security* was not mentioned once! Whatever document you are referring to, though it is often called a strategic business plan, you will normally find a vision, a mission, and a quality statement, followed by a long report that declares, without surprise, that the purpose of the organization is to make huge profits in the few (traditionally 5) years to come.

From this vague statement—vague in terms of security, of course—one has to infer a security strategic plan that fits with the core values of the company. This sometimes requires some sort of a creative approach.

But first of all, let us try to extract critical success factors from strategic goals.

Core Values

As mentioned earlier, there are three components in the CSFs. Each component is differently disposed to measurement. Core values, for example, are hardly tangible, nor are they prone to being measured on any kind of scale. Yet, their importance is crucial. The corporate culture can be observed and differentiated form others, and yet it can hardly be quantified. Core values are not about quantity but about quality; they are statements, wishes, and attitudes. They are often defined by adjectives such as *dynamic*, *pioneering*, and *high-end*, which look quite nice in a frame on the wall, but do not mean much in reality. Sometimes companies issue core beliefs such as focusing on customers, promoting a safe and healthy working environment, encouraging people, empowering our people and encouraging their growth, and so on. This is very nice and one can understand why chairpersons and CEOs agree to sign these glorious statements. I have also seen organizations describe their values in writing, which is always good and will make your task easier. One company in the UAE that I know of selected five items to affirm their core values: (1) corporate reputation, (2) distinction and success, (3) leadership and teamwork, (4) strategic partnership and quality, and (5) customer service.

These core values should be the starting point of your strategic reflexion. They will help you define the competencies that are needed to do the job.

Core Competencies

The core competencies are located a bit higher on the measurability scale. They are directly linked to the mission of the company and therefore are somewhat tangible. If your company produces something (core competency) in a certain spirit and environment (core values) you should be able to extract some tangible factors such as the competencies that are needed. With this, it is now easier to outline the profile of those who will do the work, meaning that recruitment needs and expectations can be established. Once your recruitment expectations are established, you can determine what kind of training will be necessary. You can create a training program for new employees to acquire new competencies—in addition to those skills they already possess—within the core value framework. This is good. But it does not say in practical terms how you extract these needs.

Key Result Areas

Key result areas are these areas of your scope that will be given priority over others. It may be things like access control, policies and procedures, physical security, traffic control, travel security, VIP protection, or parking discipline. They stem from the global strategic plan for the organization, and/or are the result of discussions you had with your superiors and the executive suite when you were recruited. Never forget what was said then, because the reason behind your appointment is a consequence of a dissatisfaction regarding certain aspects of security in the company and is still there while you acquaint yourself with your new job. What was told to you there is probably written nowhere in your job description but ranks high in the way the management will judge your performance.

Now, how you will prioritize these KRAs remains your choice but I would suggest drafting a list of these KRAs and submitting it for approval to your hierarchy. You may have surprises, and it is best to start out on the right foot with clear tasks ahead. When you start performing, you create a momentum that is difficult to stop or divert.

I suggest now that you create a table to summarize your reflections so far. The table would look like this:

Critical Success Factors		
Key Result Areas	**Core Competencies**	**Core Values**
		Customer focused
		Empowering
		Committed
Total	**Total:**	**Total:**

You need a bit of imagination to fill out the table. Let us take an example:

The company ABC lists the following values in their strategic business plan

- Our values are to be open minded, flexible, empowering, encouraging, and committed to our employees and customers. These core values should appear in the right column of the table.
- What core competencies can you deduce from these core values that relate to security?

I believe that you are now facing a complex task that you may not be able to fix by yourself. How can you link open-mindedness and flexibility to elements of an asset protection program? You have several solutions. The first one involves thinking by yourself and having your findings validated by your security team. Another one is to put your closest staff in a room, lock the door, and try to find responses. But you may have only one or two cadres to help you. Another one is to go for the twenty-idea method proposed by Dobbins and Pettman (2006: 18):

1. Write down the problem/challenge/opportunity. In our case what are the core competencies stemming from our core values?
2. Generate twenty possible answers.
3. Select the appropriate answer and take immediate action.

Sounds too simple to be true? The secret in this method is that it seems that answers seventeen through twenty often prove to be the best ones. This is why it is crucial to go right to the twentieth.

In our simple example, we have first to transform values into core competencies. Let us start with customer focused. What can you infer from that simple idea? It means that your organization is focused on giving satisfaction to customers. To achieve this means making sure that orders are safely *produced* and products *delivered on time* to the customers in a *quick, effective, and friendly* way. Could we say that writing that the products are produced safely and on time means that no interference such as a security incident comes to disrupt the production process? This, in turn, indicates that the tools of production must be protected and that the people who operate these tools should be able to do so without security concerns. What can we infer from this in terms of core competencies? We could say that the organization needs to make sure that access is given only to legitimate employees (access control system for employees and vehicles, background checks—HR security—strict work permits for contractors, visitor procedures, etc.), that their place of work should be secure (i.e., the whole gamut of physical security measures to protect the organization's production lines need to be implemented: CCTV cameras, physical barriers, alarms, and that these people have a fair idea of what their security duties are in this context and which behaviors are acceptable and which ones are not [awareness program for employees and policies and procedures]).

From this simple *customer focused*, we managed to generate an almost acceptable security plan which was far from being obvious when we started thinking.

If we now use the same thinking process for the word *empowering* we will probably obtain the same core competencies and add a few others. For example, if the organization considers empowering employees as part of the overall philosophy, people should be able to develop in their work framework in order to progress in their career, correct? We have to repeat then the same necessity to work in a safe and secure framework and add a few things that may be a result of my own extrapolation tendency. People who commit to their company and have the opportunity to be empowered may tend to work harder, and perhaps longer hours. This means that the security before and after hours should be of the same quality as during office hours, because people may come early and leave late. You now have to take into account the security of the building before hours (procedures about the cleaning staff, including clean desk policy) along with the security of the parking lot before and after hours (CCTV surveillance, lighting, patrolling patterns, First-Aid course, etc.). One can see from these examples that one can extrapolate reasonably and justify the creation/ existence/adjustment of a classic assets protection program and be able to justify the measures as being in line with the vision, mission statements, and values of the company. Once you have listed all these elements, and there might be many of them, in fact as many as the expected number of headings in a security master plan (and even a crisis emergency plan, or a business continuity plan, although these plans are a bit outside the traditional scope of work of security executives). Therefore, from a few simple values one is able to draw a list of core competencies that will need to be developed in the organization. These core competencies will be used in a training and development program where they will be measured against the existing capabilities of both the work force and the security department. Now, let us discuss the key result areas issue.

WHY THESE KEY RESULTS AREAS?

Now that you have listed the core competencies, the most delicate task is selecting the KRAs, or the areas of security that need to be prioritized. Although you will have noted the management requirements, these requirements should not systematically be taken at face value. Most of the time, they are emotional reactions to episodes that displeased the management. When the GM one of the organization I worked for told me how impressed he had been when visiting the headquarters of a French company in La Défense, where security, he said, "is first class and at the same time nowhere to be seen!" I did not mention then that the vision of a security officer should not be so indisposing to any employee—as it sometimes is—nor that security was so invisible because the security was acting one floor below and that CCTV surveillance was constant with needle-sized cameras all over the lobby, with a quick reaction team ready to intervene to the slightest alarm, or any other issues. The translated requirement here was: I do not want to see security people around, I find their presence unsettling, and employees do not want to see them—find a way to make them transparent. Such a thing is never very pleasant to hear, and even more difficult to convey to the officers in question!

The logical deduction from this discussion was that security guards should not be conspicuously deployed, even during rush hours, and that they should make themselves scarce. The measures I took were first to change the uniforms from a traditional para-military uniform to a blazer, grey slacks, and company tie; make better use of CCTV; and make the monitoring of the surveillance system a stronger part of my security plan. Although this did not change the attitude of the management toward the security department, it seemed to stop criticism. The number of acting officers was still the same, but because they acted mainly behind monitors and in offices, it seemed to improve their relationship with the workforce.

Reflect on what managers have told you and try to synthetize their demands into a spirit that should drive your decisions. It is with this spirit in mind—somehow the core values of management regarding security— that you should create and prioritize your KRAs.

I do not really have a secret recipe to prioritize your actions, but I can suggest a few ideas. You could prioritize according to:

- Security weaknesses that you have witnessed since you arrived and that you know need urgent fixing
- Spectacular actions that would put you and your department at the center of conversations: a double-edged sword
- Mild security changes that will not upset the workforce or the management and that will instill a cooperative spirit in the employees and the management alike
- Immediate actions that will comply with the top-management demands at the risk of alienating the employees

It would appear quite logical to apply the principles discussed in Chapter 3 about the management of change. Read the chapter carefully and then make your choices according to what you want as a manager. Get some middle managers involved, discuss issues with your peers; from your discussions with them, you will get a direction. It takes time to understand a company's culture and time is something that is in very short supply at this point. You must act quickly to make your mark on security. Just keep this important thing in mind: Your choices should reflect your personality. Do not let yourself be driven by your deputies in a direction you might later regret. You are a certain type of person, and I suggest your implementation choices reflect the person you are. If you are a dynamic, no-nonsense person who is attached to getting quick results, people from the executive suite to the security officer will expect you to behave like a hussar. If you are a rather thoughtful, mild-tempered, and friendly person, start slowly with changes in policies and with awareness sessions in order to make people adhere to the changes, because they feel you are a likeable person and that you do what is good for the organization. The time factor also has to be present in your equation. If management wants quick results, you may have to force your nature and act more assertively/aggressively than you would like. The equation is complex and you must therefore find a solution tailored to your situation.

Once you have listed and prioritized your key result areas it is time to start building the famous key performance indicators that everybody is expecting you to deliver and that are perceived as the miracle solution to measure (and improve) performance.

KEY PERFORMANCE INDICATORS

Defining key performance indicators is quite simple really. KPIs are quantitative targets that need to be reached within a time span in a selected key result area.

KPIs are rates, ratios, averages, or percentages that reflect (or measure) the status of the critical success factors (CSFs) of an organization.

Principle for Creating KPIs

When you create a KPI, you must bear in mind three important things. A KPI should: (1) reflect critical success factors, (2) be quantifiable, and (3) be linked to business goals.

KPIs must also be based on observed measurements, which reflect the security posture of the company in different security areas. The KPI aims to measure but also to improve this security posture.

Example of KPI Construction

To achieve success, it is important to translate KRAs and KPIs into goals, targets, and deadlines. The principle to build a KPI is as follows:

1. Select the KRA (e.g., access control during peak time).
2. Select the KPI goal (full control of entries at HQ main gate).
3. Select the target (95% of correct entries for year 1).
4. Select a deadline (by 31 December 2019).
5. Link them in a statement.

KPI: *Improve access control at headquarters by bringing the percentage of lawful entries at the main gate to 95% by 31 December 2019* (Figure 4.2).

Below are a few examples of KPIs construction (Figure 4.3).

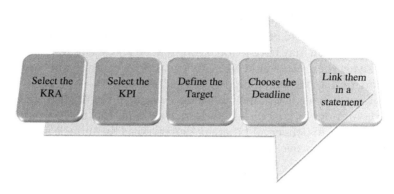

Figure 4.2 The KPI construction process.

Key performance indicators must be applied in areas of the security department that are part of their annual business plan and objectives. Further to what I said earlier in this chapter, you may choose to make specific efforts in certain areas of security that we have called key results areas.

KPIs will reflect the concerns of the management, and the necessity to align with the strategic business objectives of the organization. Key result areas may have been determined for a number of reasons. They could be:

- The necessity to align security initiatives with business strategic objectives
- The desire to make some areas of security more prominent and effective
- A request from the top management
- New security regulations emanating from overarching authorities (organization HQ, national standards and regulations, a new partner's standards further to merger, etc.)
- A necessity to bring these areas to a specific standard

The KPIs are divided into *leading* KPIs which are areas where the security section has control and can influence the performance (*own actions*), and *lagging* KPIs which are areas where the security department has no control and over which it has limited influence (*actions by employees*).

Key performance indicators must reflect security goals and objectives that need to be monitored for improvement by the security department (Figure 4.4). Based on the organization's strategic objectives issued

KRA	KPI Objective	Target	Date	Key Performance Indicator
Access Control	Ensure that the badge system works satisfactorily	2% incident at HQ entry during morning peak hours	December 2019	Improve access control reliability by reaching a 2% maximum incident occurrence at HQ during morning peak time by December 2019
Security Awareness and Training	Ensure that all employees have heard about social engineering; to this effect plan 12 security awareness and training (SAT) sessions	25% of the organization HQ attend an awareness session about social engineering	December 2019	By December 2019, 25% of all personnel will have attended a social engineering SAT session at HQ
Surveys and Risk Management	Create a pool of security professionals that can perform security risk assessment (SRA) for the organization and their overseas offices	Train at least 5 SRA professionals in the company	January 2020	By the end of January 2020, 5 SRA practitioners, 3 in our office in London and 2 in our office in Houston, will have been trained

Figure 4.3 Examples of KPI construction.

every year, security performance management will be based on the following approach:

1. Develop the right metrics to drive the right security behavior toward the organization's strategy.
2. Set ambitious yet realistic targets on KPIs. Key performance indicators will be defined by: (1) an action, (2) some figures (e.g., numbers, ratios, or percentages), and (3) a deadline. *Any KPI without these three elements is not a KPI.*

Figure 4.4   The KPI management process.

3. Track performance against targets at all levels of the security organization.
4. Create dialogue when off target.
5. Take corrective action.

The SMART Criteria Applied to KPIs

The SMART criteria must be applied when defining KPIs. Questions should be asked in order to build relevant KPIs. The following guidelines aim to provide some help for the building of significant KPIs. KPIs should be:

Specific

This means that although a key result area can be measured through four or five KPIs, KPIs address one single issue at a time. This issue must be clearly defined and must, with the objective and the deadline, form a coherent whole. One KPI = one issue, one target, one deadline.

The questions to answer are the following:

- How challenging will it be? An unreasonable target, a far too close deadline will make your KPI irrelevant. Looking for the perfect outcome to a long-established problem will not be taken seriously and will damage your credibility. Base your KPIs on known metrics from previous years that you want to improve.

- How will it compare with last year? This is really what matters. You must be audacious to show that your department sets high targets and that you are ready to tackle security problems that you deem solvable. Of course, if you do not have metrics to set up your goals, you cannot do much except collect figures that will be used next year to build the first set of KPIs.
- Is benchmarking an option? And if it is, which benchmarks could be used? Benchmarking is good, provided you have access to broadly comparable and equally relevant data. If you come from a position comparable to the one you just got, in a similar or at least comparable industry, this is fine, you can benchmark against that, and see where you can improve the existing situation. If you are new to both the position and the business you are now protecting, trying to benchmark will be very time consuming in meetings and in visits and may not really help you much. By experience, you start to benchmark with peers when you really master your environment and this takes time, a commodity you seldom have when you prepare your initial security master plan.
- What kind of improvement does this represent for the department/ team? This is an important point to consider of course. This is the what's in it for me from your colleagues in the security force. If you want your people to support your initiatives, there must be something in for them. It can be training, it can be prestige, exciting new work, the possibility to be deployed elsewhere, the opportunity to sit certifications, and so on.
- Does it contribute to the unit's objectives? Always keep in mind that when you plan security initiatives they must benefit the following units in this order: (1) you, (2) the security department, (3) the workforce, and (4) the executive management. I know that many will disagree with my ranking, reversing the priorities, but I stick to it, although I did not apply it that way during my career. We will discuss this issue later in Chapter 6.
- Does it aid the individual's personal development? This is a consequence of the previous point. When you improve security, you create new tasks, which in turn necessitate new skills. New skills mean new training, and training means an important vector of motivation for your guard force. You must try to keep this momentum of new

tasks, new skills to acquire, new training, and a motivated guard force at all time. It is quite easy when you upset the existing system, but you must keep your guard force on their toes if you want them to perform and consequently be proud of themselves and their jobs.

Measurable (Qualitative)

There are two ways to measure performance, qualitative and quantitative. Many people think that quantitative performance is the only way to convince the management of the effectiveness of the security program and tend to focus on measurable things. In political science, doing so is called a numerical fallacy. It does not mean that it is useless, on the contrary, but focusing on measurable things may divert you from your paramount goal, which is to improve the security posture of your company. To me, the epitome of success is to have a security program endorsed by all in the organization. And this is hardly quantifiable. If you manage to transform the perception of security from one of constraints and restriction to the image of security as the main business enabler, you have succeeded. What this entails is, somehow, measuring the feelings of the staff and management toward your action.

How Can Quality Be Measured?

This is an interesting question and I have explored a few publications to find inspiration. I found nothing really convincing, because as I said, in business, and security is a business unit, there is an overwhelming trust in figures. This is why risk assessments are full of figures that reflect, most of the time, feelings disguised as scientific evaluations. Intuitive feelings look best when draped in figures. It makes the consultant look very competent but this is some kind of a deception, really. I know this is the only way to make calculations and that this is why figures are used instead of words, but still there is nothing scientific in it and we do not really warn our customer about that, do we?

Be that as it may, quality must and can be measured. What do I mean by qualitatively measuring the security performance? It means measuring the quality if what is being done: monitoring accesses, overall perimeter surveillance, management of badges, security awareness sessions, patrolling—all these actions are done according to the security plan and are perceived as being beneficial to the posture of the organization and the security of the workforce. The best way to certify that this is the case is through an external audit. How should this audit proceed? I think that if you want to make sure that the security program is good and genuinely endorsed by the workforce, the best thing to do is to ask them.

I think that asking the employees their opinion about the work of the security department is the right way to qualitatively measure the performance of security.

Security Audit on Quality Performance

An audit of the security program can also be performed with an exhaustive security list, which considers all aspects of security. Several books offer quite comprehensive lists (e.g., Perois 2016) and these lists should be studied and adapted to the nature of your business. The principle behind this is that you should perform these audits on a regular basis in order to be able to get statistics that are relevant.

I suggest one, not really scientific, but acceptable, way of doing this in a corporate context. Let us say that you select 20 questions on physical security that need to be answered positively. During your initial survey, the workforce provides an average of 12 positive answers out of 20, from which you could say that you have a 60% level of satisfaction with your internal customers in that specific domain (e.g., physical security). The following year, you perform a new survey and happen to have 80% positive replies. You can therefore say that you have increased the perception of the security posture of the company by 20% in 1 year. Although it is not perfect, because you may not have asked all the right questions, and your questionnaire is biased one way or another, it allows you to make statements—how good you will be at making these statements will be important—about the overall security posture of the organization, the increasing support of the workforce for these changes, and the work achieved by your department. It is imperative to give figures to the management and they must be as explicit as possible. Of course, for your results to be exploitable, you need to ask the same questions every time; otherwise, how could you measure performance and progress? Your questions should be right (or as right as possible) from their inception, and be sufficiently generic to be used repeatedly. This is not simple, because a security program is a work in progress and while the program evolves, so will the questions to ask, which will reflect the change in performance. You should therefore maintain part of the questions as inalterable (those regarding the feelings of security and safety felt by the employees) and others more technical that will change every year and that will be used statistically when compared to one another. I believe that showing that there is a growing confidence between the workforce and the security department is central to the security issue, because it shows that security is working in line with the core values of the organization.

The Security Survey and Questionnaire

Another very important issue is linked to the concept of change. As we saw in the previous chapter, managing change is paramount in your program implementation, and the purpose of change management is to have your security program accepted and endorsed by those for whom it was written. I see two ways of measuring performance for the same issue. A quantitative way would be to ask whether all permanent employees are wearing their badges during office hours. This can be quantitatively measured through a security audit. The qualitative approach would be to ask whether employees feel that their security at work has been improved through wearing a badge at work. This would be the qualitative aspect of the same issue, measured emotionally rather than through arithmetic. Both questions deal with the badge issue and yet they reflect two different things. One is about a procedure to follow, and how it is followed, and the other deals with the acceptance—once could say the success—of the implementation of such a procedure. To me, both are equally important and both should be measured. These questions could be part of the security survey, but as I said in the previous section, it is not easy to keep identical question audit after audit. This is why I suggest an option that I have not personally tested but of which I have heard only good things: Prepare an electronic survey focusing on the perception of security by the employees. Your questions will be about the way security is organized in the company, their experience with it, whether they feel safe and secure, and whether they support/endorse the program. Personally, I use Survey Monkey for all my surveys (I started during my PhD research and maintained my subscription with them, something I do not regret). The first questionnaire is a bit difficult to put together, but even if you are not an IT genius, it is manageable with the help of computer-savvy people in the office. When you are stuck the people at Survey Monkey are really helpful! Focus on these areas:

1. Organization of security
2. Perception of security
3. Personal experience of security
4. Feeling of safety/security in the working environment
5. Ways to improve security (suggestions by the employees)

Prepare this survey with great care. Do not make it too long and use closed questions (answer YES or NO, except for the suggestion question; people hate being asked to write what they think or feel in an empty box—at least most of us). Keep the number of questions manageable if you want to create statistics. And make sure that these questions can be used several times. What you want to be able to demonstrate is something like this:

In 2018, 54% of the workforce felt safe overall at the office. In 2019, this figure increased to 78%.

Such a demonstration has, of course, only a relative value, unless you can complement it with another statement that says security measures implemented recently have increased the security of the personnel while at the same time production increased by, say, 12%. This game with percentages is what you should aim for, if you want to be read with interest by the C-suite. Keep it simple, always. I know that HSE people, the kings of pies, inundate management with charts, pies, and graphs, but personally, I never checked those types of graphs in detail and I suspect the guys on the executive floor do the same. I prefer ratios and percentages that stick in my mind and are easy to remember.

The Influence Indicators

Campbell, in the excellent *Measures and Metrics in Corporate Security* (2007), published by the Security Executive Council, proposes a Security Program Legitimacy Index (SPLI) that provides a list of questions to ascertain senior management's confidence in the security function and the legitimacy of the highest security personnel—CSO, VP of security, director. He warns that the list should be adapted to the culture of your organization and that it should be verified by knowledgeable and objective peers and superiors (Campbell 2007: 42). This table should be filled in by you, the security executive. As such it will probably be biased, but again, bias is inevitable and we must live with it. I reproduce this table here. Yours may be slightly different but the spirit should be kept (Table 4.1).

These 12 indicators should provide you with a good idea about the strength of your soft power in the organization. It is good to keep this in mind and reassess your situation annually. Things change positively, but also in a negative direction. Keep records of this Legitimacy Index.

Measurable (Quantitative)

The quantitative part of the performance measurement seems quite straightforward. In reality, it is a bit complicated. There is the risk of considering only what can be measured at the expense of what cannot be measured easily. The second danger is to use figures in isolation, a mistake

Table 4.1   The Security Program Legitimacy Index

Security Program Legitimacy Index (SPLI)

Rate 1 (low) to 5 (high) your confidence that the statement applies to your organization.	1–5

Operational effectiveness. There is clear evidence that security programs work to protect the enterprise and its people and create respect and support for those programs and security leadership.

The CSO has unhindered access to the top. The boss knows who you are and answers the phone when you call.

Corporate security can influence the strategic direction of the business. Security has to be an enabler of business success and competitiveness. If you make it less risky to do business, you are contributing to the bottom line in real numbers and giving the business an edge.

Corporate security is an acknowledged stakeholder in the corporate risk management program. The CSO has a well-placed chair at the risk management and corporate governance table.

When security issues are escalated, there are no surprises. This is another view of access but keyed to by passing the guy who says, "Don't tell the boss." Delivering bad news goes with the job.

Management connects security's program with value delivered. Business leadership connects a value (competitive, risk avoidance, personal safety, etc.) to security programs and operations.

Senior management responds appropriately to security's proposals. The CSO knows how to sell the program and top management listens. This does not mean unquestioned or 100% acceptance.

Senior management exhibits clear support of security policy. The CSO has articulated a risk-responsive set of high-level policy statements that top management understands and supports with resources and reinforcements.

Security has sufficient resources to accomplish the protection mission. Your programs are deemed worth the price. Sufficient to deliver on the policies, not excessive or gold-plated.

Security's programs have a positive impact on the ethical hygiene of the firm. Security's programs and leadership reinforce the culture of doing the right thing and deliver key services in support of the system of internal controls. Moreover, customers have high confidence in security's attention to their concerns and in the integrity of its people and operations.

(Continued)

Table 4.1 (*Continued*)   The Security Program Legitimacy Index

Security Program Legitimacy Index (SPLI)
The CSO exercises exclusive ownership of the firm's security program. This envisions all security services under one executive, the CSO, but may also be served by the CSO chairing a security committee comprised of all related services and other members of the governance infrastructure.
Security's customer base exhibits broad knowledge of security program components and risk awareness. A key indicator that the CSO knows how to reach people and influence behavior and individual responsibility. Security has successfully sold the notion that the maintenance of security is a shared responsibility with employees and business management.

I have seen in many reports. Figures have value only when related to the bigger picture. A KPI must be a rate, a ratio, an average, or a percentage of something to tell tales. It must measure the status of the critical success factors discussed earlier. Its construction must be done with care. Collective thought—you and your security cadres, if you have any—may give improved results.

Also, bear in mind that figures must highlight the role security plays in the overall business capability of the organization. They must show that thanks to you, the potential threats facing the organization are controlled and as a result the organization remains competitive. This is what the executive suite wants to see and this what you must aptly demonstrate.

There are excellent books on metrics measurement and these books will discuss at great length the way to measure incidents and unwanted security events. But what is paramount here is to understand the core values of the organization and choose metrics that fit this approach.

If your company is selling services, there will be specific incidents that you want to prevent absolutely such as workplace violence, laptop thefts, company contract leaks, and sharing of any other documents that need not to be known or discovered by third parties. If your factory is producing finished products, you may fear product being stolen, fabrication secret leaks, or the theft of any valued raw material.

At that stage, it might be a good starting point to create a risk inventory.

THE RISK INVENTORY

The purpose of the risk inventory is to identify potential threats your organization might face as well as their attached vulnerabilities in order to devise a list of countermeasures to mitigate the risks. The risk inventory is not specific to the organization but rather to the units that compose it. The list of risks facing headquarters will differ from the list of risks facing the factory or the pipeline that runs from one facility to another.

As the example below will demonstrate, headquarters has specific threats centered around theft, including trade secret theft and embezzlement; payroll fraud; workplace violence; parking violations; cyberattacks and property thefts; phishing; and social engineering. Your field facility could be a victim of theft (raw material and finished products), that is, unlawful penetration on site such as sabotage of the supervisory control and data acquisition (SCADA) system or drug and alcohol smuggling.

Each of these risks can be associated with undesired security events that need to be (1) defined, (2) understood, and (3) quantified.

CASE STUDY 1: RECURRENT PETTY THEFT IN THE OFFICE

Let us review a quick case study about recurrent theft in offices. A record of private thefts would orientate the KPI toward the following KRAs (to name the most obvious): (1) Access and movement control, (2) Electronic surveillance, (3) Personnel recruitment, (4) Security awareness regarding taking care of one's belongings, and (5) Patrolling.

Let us examine them in turn. Recurrent theft may be the result of undesired visitors entering the place to steal without security being aware of the trespass. This means that access control must be tightened, and that electronic devices should be considered or upgraded.

Forensics security is quite good when it comes to theft or vandalism. I have seen surveillance at work, and it works. A situation such as recurrent petty theft means that the existing surveillance might have to be upgraded and that a surveillance plan should be put in place to face this specific threat (similar to the one you find in hotels where elevators and corridors are systematically covered). Another issue is the possibility that an employee from another area or another floor moves undetected to a specific hunting ground. This possibility points toward a movement surveillance system that could be achieved through a badging system per floor or areas, a camera outside each elevator, and so on. I know, the invoice amount is increasing at a dangerous speed, but I am just demonstrating the thinking, not justifying the budget. If you expand the thinking a little bit more, it may also point to a third KRA, the recruitment of personnel. We ignore whether the thieves are visitors or employees, but chances are that employees are the culprits, as they know the place, they know where to find things (and they have had time to identify various prey), and they know the timing habits of fellow employees. It is not unusual in the GCC countries, probably some of the safest places on earth, to see women abandoning their bags wide open on their desk, sometimes with their wallet on top of the bag, while going to the cafeteria for lunch. In such places where theft is totally unexpected and unaccepted, this points toward another area that borders on security. Perhaps if dishonest people had not been hired in the organization, theft would not have occurred. Maybe some background checks should be entrusted to security to make sure that employees are who they say they are and that their resumes tell the right tale. Such an action may be wishful thinking, though. I never had the chance to do HR security, but HR managers do not react nicely to such suggestions and want to prevent anyone from encroaching on their territory. But again, I am demonstrating a logic. Another KRA that stems from the simple observation of theft is that some security awareness sessions about the importance of looking after one's belongings and of being a bit more vigilant could lower the opportunities for crime and therefore contribute to better security—and a better atmosphere—in the organization.

CASE STUDY 2: TAILGATING AND PIGGYBACKING

Many places suffer from a tailgating and piggybacking culture/problem. Doss (2011) defines *piggybacking* as occurring when an "unauthorized or 'known' individual follows [an] authorized user into a secured facility or area without using his/her proper credential." A good example of this is when two employees return from lunch and only one employee uses his access card to open the door for both employees to enter. *Tailgating* is when an unauthorized or "unknown" individual follows an authorized person into a facility or area (Doss 2011: 7–3).

Tailgating creates a number of security problems, the first one being that it nullifies the value of sophisticated electronic systems (unless coupled with CCTV cameras covering the gates, which is fortunately often the case). Tailgaters could be anyone from thieves to disgruntled employees or simply employees verging on the dishonest (chancers or opportunists?). Most of the time, they are only lazy employees who do not want to look for their access badge or who left the badge on their desk when they went out. A simple basic issue such as tailgating may drive your reflection toward the following potential issues. Here we see that the access control key result area can be served by five KPIs:

- Employee security awareness (KPIs would discuss the number of awareness sessions to be developed during the year and the number of people who attended the sessions measured against the number of tailgating incidents).
- Adequacy of physical security features against tailgating (consider photo sensors, turnstiles, laser sensors, or mantraps to limit entry to a single person at a time and measure their efficiency; then the number of tailgating incidents could be measured against a certain period of time).
- Necessity to upgrade the badging system and the badging itself (this measure could be taken separately or as part of the previous series).
- The necessity of reassessing and probably upgrading video surveillance (here, we point to an inefficient video surveillance that can be due to either faulty/poorly installed equipment or to lousy and/or improvable post-orders). Whatever the culprit, video surveillance needs to be improved and this improvement has to be measured. For example, the number of incidents recorded in a definite period of time should show an increase and demonstrate the value of the upgraded VASS (video assessment and surveillance system).
- Training security officers to the specific tasks of access control. Although this seems difficult to translate into a KPI, the training of security officers in the handling of the morning access control could be turned into a KPI, with a bit of imagination. What is a bit controversial is that a better trained security guard force will have a positive effect on the behavior of some unruly workers, which means that the number of tailgating attempts will quickly decrease. The number of tailgating incidents recorded by the surveillance team will quickly decrease, not because of the video surveillance but because of the new attitude of the guard force. Therefore, it may not be a good idea to justify the VASS expense by measuring the decreasing number of attempts, since they are going to drop quickly for two reasons: (1) the assertive behavior of the security

officers and (2) the return on investment of the first few security awareness sessions. The other way would be to present the project as a global improvement and put everything under a single heading. This is not important right now, but it highlights the fact that you must really take this KPI selection very seriously and make sure that they do not end up contradicting your initial purpose.

Measurable (Financial)

We have already mentioned it at length, and anybody who has worked in security knows this, but security is perceived as a cost center and this image is somehow suffocating the profession. We have dedicated and competent personnel, remarkable and incredibly performing equipment, and a wealth of knowledge in the organization of security, and yet, our image is not satisfactory. CEOs are reluctant to invest in security, at least until a serious incident changes the situation. In the executive management mind, there are four questions that need to be answered when you propose to increase the security posture:

1. How much will this cost?
2. How much will it save?
3. Is a budget needed?
4. What resources are required?

How Much Will It Cost?

Often, the security consultant is not a technician, and originates from either a military/police background or an academic background (e.g., international relations, international security, politics, government studies) where the price of a camera remains an absolute mystery. This will probably change with the arrival of young graduates from security programs around the world, but I am not sure that the pricing of security features is discussed at all at the undergraduate level. There are so many other things to learn and security people are so eager to give their profession a reputation for excellence that practical things such as technical capabilities and specifications tend to be despised. This is really where most of us need to progress. My knowledge of the cost of equipment is so limited that it is really embarrassing and I dread being asked by clients, "Ok, this sounds like a good idea, but can we afford it?" By which they mean "How much will it cost, even approximately?" Even approximately, I usually do not have a clue.

101

And I do not think I am the only one. I think that every action you propose to, suggest to, or implement with the department should be quantifiable in terms of hard cash. First of all, it will help you understand what physical security is about. It is important, for example, when you want to recommend **pan–tilt–zoom** (PTZ) cameras instead of fixed cameras. The same goes for security and the executive suite. They cannot make the right decision when they ignore the price, and discussing the advantages of your technical solution will not register as long as they cannot link it in their mind to a cost. Money talks, they say. I prefer money decides.

Attainable/Achievable/Agreed
These three words do not mean exactly the same thing, although the first two are quite close. The questions that you must ask yourself are "Is the program—or part of it—achievable or attainable with the resources and means at my disposal?" This brings us again to the issue of budget. A budget is paramount to security implementation. When I was, for a few years, director of security of a relatively big company I had no budget on my own. Every suggestion I made was submitted to the executive committee via the VP of security and I could never defend my proposals in person which means, you guessed it, that the security program advanced more slowly than I had wanted. During my tenure there, getting frustrated, I applied for a job at a major shipping company based in Denmark. I did well on their test and was flown to Copenhagen for the final interviews (three candidates were still being considered). During my numerous interviews—Danes are very thorough in what they do—with HR staff, I insisted on the issue of budget, telling them that should my budget be administered by somebody else, I would not consider taking the job. I could see that this attitude was not appreciated and I did not get the job. I do not know whether this particular emphasis on getting my own budget was a handicap to my application, and I will never know.

Be that as it may, you will be very lucky if you have your own budget to manage, but it will also make your life very complicated, unless you have enough resources to have one of your cadres dedicated to "finding prices" and get yourself acquainted with basic figures (e.g., at some point I had a price for a kilometer of fence with detection equipment, a price for fully equipped gatehouses, etc.). Knowing these basic facts made my meetings and discussions with clients relevant and dynamic. If you are able to quote (financially) any security item you mention in a document, you will become absolutely indispensable to clients and also to your top management. You will really become a lynchpin!

Now that you have established your objectives and put them in a reasonable timeframe, you need to check whether there are any reservations about the objectives, and think about how to overcome them.

As with every project, you will have to do a SWOT exercise.

The SWOT components (strengths, weaknesses, opportunities, and threats) have already been discussed in Chapter 1 and can be obtained via a simple brainstorming exercise with your staff. You need to discuss and measure the weight of these four elements. To see whether your security program is achievable you must be conscious of the hurdles you and your team will face along the way. You must also consider your weaknesses with honesty (e.g., small budget, weaknesses in guard force competency, lack of solid procedures, cultural issues, adversarial elements). These weaknesses and threats should be counterbalanced by your strengths and the opportunities that could turn to your advantage. Your strengths can be the network and experience you, or some of your staff, bring to the organization. They can be solid existing physical security, and/or the support and commitment provided by the CEO or one of her deputies. Opportunities can be events. For example, the gas project I was working for turned from a project into an operation. This transition was marked by impressive ceremonies, with lots a VIPs and other pomp and circumstance. This event created an extraordinary opportunity to use the principles of event security and to link it to other areas of security (physical security, cooperation with local police and firefighters, renewed procedures, an emergency plan, physical security—new barriers and CCTV surveillance, X-ray machines, explosive hand-held devices—served by a guard force who had to undergo some training to be able to serve this new equipment on time, etc.). The event was a resounding success and the image of security, I guess, was enhanced in the executive suite's mind. But for me, it was a fantastic opportunity to ask for equipment that I would have obtained probably much later and in lesser numbers. Using a prestigious event as an opportunity, with the reputation of the organization at stake, was a good way to improve the security posture of the company without giving the feeling of begging for expensive and unnecessary security equipment.

Last, you need to make sure that your security program is in line with the objectives of the business. This point needs to be repeated endlessly. If you cannot justify that you are working according to the objectives and core values of the organization, you will go nowhere and your security department will remain a traditional security department, one we have seen too often and that we do not want to be responsible for. Yet, there are reasons most security departments are ruled by the guard-at-the-gate mentality. They are easy to run, expectations are low, and adverse incidents are often not even discovered. But my guess is that if you are reading this book, you want to achieve something else and be proud of your achievements. To do this, the capability to quote security items and the constant attention to business objectives are the prerequisites to strategic success.

Relevant/Realistic/Results Orientated
Three interesting Rs here. First, relevant: We again come back to the issue of having security that serves the core values of the organization. If your program is not in line with the philosophy of the top management, the workforce will resent it. It must be "in the spirit." If the atmosphere is relaxed and informal (e.g., like at IT companies), security must be discreet and unobtrusive. This does not mean that security officers do not do their work. It means they must do it differently. Uniforms, instead of being of the para-military type, should look more like what a golf player would wear (e.g., polo shirt and beige slacks). Big radios should be minimized to appear less aggressive, and so on. Military haircuts should be discouraged in the guard force. If, on the contrary, the company produces and delivers military equipment in a far-off place, a military look seems more appropriate. Use your common sense. Speak with people, use your eyes and your ears, and suggest choices. Benchmark against comparable industries in similar environments. Discuss issues with your peers and your cadres. In one of the companies I worked for, I noticed that security officers were looked down on by most employees. Therefore, the first thing I did was to dress them in blazer, grey slacks, and club ties. It immediately gave them gravitas and more power, and the perception of the men by the workforce drastically improved.

Realistic is another interesting R. Of course, it must be realistic, and must be in accordance with the threats the organization might be facing. What could realistically go wrong? What happened in the past? If you were lucky enough to talk with your predecessor before her departure, she might have told you what she tried to do and why, why some of it worked, and why some of it failed. She should have been able to give you a profile of the different populations comprising the workforce, and how each population reacted to changes in the security program.

Last, it should be result orientated. What this means is that the result should never be too far away and that although the method matters, the purpose remains crucial. Reaching the objectives must drive all your actions. Even when you have to abandon a path because you feel you may not have used the right method or approach, reorganize the implementation plan, keeping in mind the end-result key performance indicator.

Time Bound/Time Framed

A KPI is time related. An action must be achieved within a certain period, and conclusions (in the form of numbers, ratios, or percentage) should highlight the performance. The time necessary to achieve a KPI will depend basically upon two things: (1) the necessary time for the KPI to justify its existence and (2) the data collection frequency. If you have a monthly report about incidents, it may be a start to produce exploitable results. Figures will very quickly allow you to produce graphs that will say something to the reader. For quantifiable things, I guess monthly figures do well. After a few months, trends can be observed and indicate whether security is going in the right direction.

For qualitative evaluations, such as asking the workforce if security is doing their job well—an entirely subjective statement—I guess a yearly survey will render good service. The relationship between employees and security can sometimes be damaged by an unpleasant decision—often linked to parking slots or new badge requirements. You must, for opinions, adopt the long view. Furthermore, I am not sure that the management will see favorably your request to do a survey more than once a year. Yet, surveys give more than answers; for example, an increasing number of people taking the survey provides interesting information. It does not mean that people like security more—they may want to vent about something that upset them—but it shows an increase in interest in security affairs and must be presented as such. In summary, I suggest a monthly report for quantitative security incidents and an annual survey for the more global appreciation of the work of security in the organization. An example will be shown at the end of the chapter.

PRINCIPLE FOR KEEPING SECURITY STATISTICS AND KPIs

Every key result area should be measured using at least one KPI. Experienced practitioners recommend having three to five KPIs per KRA. If you have more than that, you may want to subdivide a KRA into two KRAs.

The Collection and Management of Data

One of the main issues of metrics is the collection of data. For each metric, the first decision to establish a process to collect data should be made by answering the following questions:

- What specific data will be collected?
- How will the data be collected?
- When will the data be collected?
- Who will collect the data?
- Where will the data be collected?
- What will the data depict?
- How will it be presented?
- To whom will it be presented?

Each of these questions must be given some serious thought, as they will impact the results provided. The nature of the data collected is of course paramount. And you better think hard about what needs to be collected. I have not seen many security metrics in my career, but the few I have been able to read were really unconvincing (from a manager's standpoint!). Measuring the number of people entering a plant or going through the gates or the number of keys lost or of cars incorrectly parked in the basement is not exactly the idea of a dynamic and effective security department. I do not say that these figures have no meaning. On the contrary, these figures form the foundation that will help construct KPIs and measure the impact of security on the workplace. They are clearly important, but to add value, they must be the reference point to obtain statistics, ratios, or percentages, all things that tell the management what happens in the company.

The first thing is indeed to collect basic figures, such as number of visitors, number of vehicles entering and exiting the facility. These are the referents that will help you demonstrate your added value or areas of potential improvement. Then, one must collect the information that can be measured against these basic figures. With regard to access control, for example, the following violations could be collected: (1) number of visitors found unescorted; (2) number of people caught tailgating or piggybacking; (3) how many tailgating or piggybacking incidents were due to laziness and how many were due to trespassing; (4) number of badge violations per type: no badge, wrong badge, borrowed badge, expired badge; (5) wrong material control pass per type: wrong description of contents, obsolete pass, no pass at all; (6) attempt to get confidential documents out; and (7) possession of forbidden items per type: computers, telephones, memory sticks, etc.

When it comes to physical security, the data to be collected may refer to (1) perimeter incident—the patrol has spotted evidence of human activity around the fence that may have been an attempt to penetrate the facility at that location, or to take material outside the facility without permit; (2) number of offices found unlocked at night—if the policy of the company is to lock the offices after work; and (3) suspicious activities or packages. By reading this physical security incident selection one can immediately see that to be detected—and therefore collected—there must be an obvious will to collect the data. It means that patrolling must be done regularly and seriously, by day and at night, according to a thorough pattern—I did not say a fixed pattern, but a thorough pattern where surroundings, perimeter, buildings, open spaces, parking lots, and operational areas are walked by a dedicated and dynamic guard force. The guard force must be permanently employed dynamically. There is no other way to get results.

One example? I have seen countless times CCTV surveillance operators taking their post without enthusiasm ready to spend the next 2 hours on their cell phone. Their excuse? Who can check 90 cameras at the same time? It is boring, stupid, and totally impractical. I agree and I disagree. Even if your system is equipped with alarms or video analytics and if, for the time being, the only thing you have to control the perimeter of the facility is a set of fixed cameras, there are ways and means to make the surveillance dynamic. How so? The security supervisor should prepare sequences of surveillance that the officer on duty will check every 30 minutes. Cameras will not be chosen randomly but according to the specific physical configuration of the facility. The officer goes through his list of cameras every 30 minutes and it takes him from 10 to 15 minutes to complete the sequence should everything be quiet. Then, he does not have the feeling of wasting his time. I remember once, our CCTV operator found a big box next to the fence, on the inside, that was not there 30 minutes earlier. It created of course some welcomed action and the presence of the box was quickly explained, but it showed the guard force that the sequence technique worked. This should not prevent you from requesting a perimeter alarm system (VASS or equivalent), but you can maintain a degree of alertness among your personnel. I know there does not seem to be much strategy in these reminiscences, and yet, your strategic objectives will be achieved only if you can count on your people to achieve them. To make them part of the process is strategic.

The following suggestions aim to calibrate the collection of data in the organization:

- In the case of multiple sites (facilities, headquarters, retail shops, etc.), each entity will keep record of the same security events (according to a template provided by corporate security) in order to establish consistent and meaningful statistics.
- Each security authority for each site will daily, weekly or monthly:
  - Consolidate all the reports from the officers
  - Confirm the accuracy of the data
  - Complete the summary of results
  - If skilled, provide a readable graph (pie or chart)
  - Submit the summary to the highest security authority on site before the end of their period of shift (depending on organization, this can be daily, weekly, bi-monthly, etc.)
- This report will be checked for accuracy and sometimes clarification. Once all its components (details of the incident, location, time, reaction, conclusion) are understood, it will be incorporated in a monthly security report drafted by the security director and submitted to the highest security entity (CSO or VP of security).
- This report will be a compilation of all the individual security reports collected at the facility/unit level. It will be comprised of four elements: (1) tables, (2) graphs to illustrate the results, (3) comments on the results, and (4) proposed actions/solutions with a time line.

Of course, the site security authority will use their own judgment regarding the severity or possible consequences of a security incident, and decide whether to report a specific incident to their immediate superior in order to get guidance. *Routine security incidents do not require immediate report to the next security authority.*

FEEDING THE KPIs: THE NEED FOR RELEVANT METRICS

Statistics (or ratios and percentages), and how to use them to help improve the security posture of the organization, are the drivers behind a security program, and their importance cannot be overemphasized. How statistics will be obtained needs to be clearly explained and understood by all in the security department.

KPIs, to be meaningful, need to be served by metrics that mean something. Creating metrics to support the daily routine in the security department will not add value. It will comfort the management in the idea that security officers are just bodies at the gate and an unpleasant cost center. What is crucial is to build metrics that are adequate and satisfy the needs of the organization and above all of those who run it.

But first, let us give a clear definition of what a metric is. For Kovacich, a security metric is:

> the application of quantitative, statistical and/or mathematical analyses to measuring security functional costs, benefits, successes, failures, trends and workload. (Kovacich 2006: xviii)

This is a very thorough definition of a metric and beyond the scope of this book. What I intend to discuss here is the understanding of when a security metric becomes significant to the management. What I wish to provide is reflection related to the security value of metrics to business and how they can serve your strategic objectives as head of the security department and as a security executive. But it is good to know that metrics are not only indicators of objectives and trends, but also of failures. Metrics must be used to promote the effectiveness of the security protection program you intend to implement in the organization and highlight the relationship between costs and benefits. But first, it should be used to highlight the security problems in the organization. With metrics, your demands for better security will be listened to. Metrics are basically your unique weapon.

Metrics allow the security manager to be more quantitative in his approach and express its value effectively with management. Depending on the type of metrics, the security manager can observe trends and use the metrics to adapt the security program to these trends. This, of course, might fall short of the business expectations of the executive management. Executive managers, in my experience, think this way:

- What is all this security costing me?
- Do I have the right amount of protection for the money I spend?
- How do I know that security is working?
- Can it be done for cheaper?

Answers to these questions lie in a quite complex structure called the Security Metrics Management Program and can be found in detail in Kovacich and Halibozek (see bibliography). At our level, we will stay clear of this program and suggest some examples of simple security metrics that can be used to your advantage.

DEVELOPING A SIMPLE METRICS PROGRAM

A metrics management program will require the same strategic thinking as establishing a security program. The vision, mission, and goals statements of the organization must guide you as you choose metrics. Your task as a CSO, VP of security, or security director is to choose metrics that will serve the KPIs you have been asked to create. My experience tells me that you will be asked to prepare KPIs to measure the quality of the security and its improvement.

We must first think about what our management considers to be the most important task of security. This should help you identify the key result areas, the first step of your thinking. Campbell suggests that the chief financial officer of the organization should be consulted (Campbell 2007: 57). He also suggests approaching other senior executives to discuss what they see as major risks to their operations. This is very good advice, at least in theory. Personally, I have always found it difficult to discuss security with other middle managers and almost impossible to discuss with members of the C-suite, apart from the person you report to (CSO or VP of security). Apart from a friendly chat leading nowhere, establishing real cooperation between functional departments is never easy. I may not be the best communicant, I admit, and in my corporate days I might have lacked the experience I now have. But I think it is worth a try. It is important to know what your peers think of their own security, and their ideas will often surprise you positively and give you ideas.

If the problems you are facing are not always *security only* problems, the solution may also be only partially a security solution. Often, the fears of your peers should be addressed through business continuity rather than security, and if you have a BC specialist in the company, you would be well advised to work a few common metrics with him.

Often, significant metrics will bring in their wake BC, safety, HR and cybersecurity issues. As in academia, topics are never clear-cut and you will find yourself on the edge of other managers' realm. You may be unable to articulate significant metrics without the help of these specialists. You may want to propose metrics that can be populated by departments other than security proper. This overlapping of metrics will certainly improve your image and will give you a manager's aura that may well come in handy at some later stage. Internal auditors may also be a source of reflection, and you should meet them and see what metrics could stem from their audits. As Campbell astutely writes:

> Internal audit routinely uncovers vulnerabilities that contribute to risk and are also reflected in security incidents. This is specially the case with data security, information protection, physical and logical access control, fraud risk and business recovery planning. (Campbell 2007: 57)

Before you start finalizing your metric program, you must cast a wide net. You may not receive the support you would like, but at least you must try to establish some sort of relationship with your peers and colleagues. This is important.

Now we turn to the approach of selecting metrics. There are at least two ways to think about these metrics. One is a top-to-bottom approach (think about what your boss expects from security), and the other is a security function approach, that is, start from security functions and find a way to measure their current status and address their potential improvement.

The Top-to-Bottom Approach

The first approach could be summarized in the following question from your supervisor: *How can I prove that the organization is more secure than it was last year at this time?* To answer this question, you must understand what the top management want. If they are worried about their reputation, telling them that the number of people parking illegally has decreased by 10% since you took office will probably not impress them. One should not neglect intangible factors because they usually have very tangible effects. What are the elements that they consider to measure the power and status of your organization and how security contributes to it?

Second, you must consider how this same supervisor will measure your performance. I give you one example: In a company I worked for, the management had terrible attendance issues with proprietary security officers recruited locally. Their absenteeism was simply indecent. They simply did not show up at work and never justified their absences. In other circumstances, they would have been sacked but in the cultural context of the example, there was a scheme imposed by the authorities to recruit locals for unskilled jobs—security is often considered to be an unskilled job—and it was obviously not a success. Integrating local security officers into a major local project was politically important and was one of the things top management focused on. Because security, as has already been said, was perceived as a perfect dump for unskilled laborers, it was thought it would be the perfect way to increase the number of local employees without damaging production. The issue quickly became a general embarrassment and the management turned toward the security director to obtain results. Yet, objectively, it was not really a security issue—rather it was an HR problem—nor was it endangering production. What happened in practical terms was that the security manager had a force of external security guards—that a local security provider was more than happy to deploy at short notice and exorbitant price—come every morning to fill the gaps of the no-shows. The company could afford the extra cost. But in the context in question, it was a thorny issue that touched a very raw nerve, namely the capability of locally recruited people to perform a particular job. Choosing a metric that would measure the attendance of the local employees—even if it would not have improved the security posture of the company in any way—would have been an important metric and could have been selected for that reason only. The solution to this whole issue was simple really; it was all about training these local employees. But the management could not accept the idea of paying to train a force of unskilled people performing what they thought were unskilled jobs. In other words, the security manager had the security solution to a political problem and selecting metrics that would serve this purpose was crucial.

What is important is to always keep in mind that what matters to the executive management must matter to you! You will be judged according to what they see as important. Understanding this is therefore imperative. A word of caution, though, about politically sensitive issues and cross-function metrics. Both are dangerous grounds for you, particularly if you are new with the organization. Some metrics are better left untouched/ignored and simply discussed with the management. When a topic is touchy, discuss it face to face with your supervisor rather than send a report to the whole management. Also be very cautious if you create cross-function metrics that involve other managers. Always think about the consequences your report may engender. Take responsibility for incidents you report, but keep your middle management colleagues away from any blame. If they agreed to help you create a significant metric, their efforts should not backfire subsequent to any negative repercussions and threaten their position. Keep in mind that everything you write has political consequences, for you and others, and consider these consequences before you dispatch any security report to your hierarchy.

The Security Program Approach

You can also configure metrics on the basis of an existing or planned security program. The elements of the security program need to be analyzed first. You could approach the security program from two sides. One would be to extract the metrics from the classical security function—detect, deter, delay, and respond—to which some authors add deny and recover. Having these four to six headings should help you cover most of the security program and help you think about what significant metrics would be. In some organizations, recommendations are satisfactorily organized according to this structure. Personally, I prefer to use a different approach by splitting the security program into four headings: (1) organizational security, (2) procedural security, (3) technical security, and (4) physical security.

Organizational Security

These are all the recommendations dealing with the organization of the security, for example, number, nature, and designation of the guard force; its deployment roles and the management of incidents; the principles behind the site access control; the zoning of the area into different levels of risk; the security role of employees working on site; and the security awareness sessions that would help reduce the risk exposure.

Procedural Security

These measures include those that refer to policies, plans, procedures, job descriptions, and post-orders, the latter including a number of security processes (approaching a car; requesting papers; doing a random search of people, cars, or trucks; or reacting to incidents and the staff's reporting chain). Procedural security also deals with the "what if" situations a security officer could face. Training forms the backbone of its implementation.

Technical Security

Technical security encompasses anything that needs power to function: access control, CCTV, automatic licence plate recognition (ALPR), under vehicle inspection system (UVIS), microwave or infrared detection systems, fiberoptic cables, lighting, radar, badging systems, road blockers, and guard tour systems, to name a few.

Physical Security

Physical security (stone and steel and no power) consists of gates, fences, walls, gatehouses, vehicle crash barriers, concertinas, jersey barriers, and so on. Physical security is where the principles of crime prevention through environmental design (CPTED) can be applied with success, reducing the cost of technical security.

No one approach covers the entirety of a security program, and my approach is rather physical security oriented because this is what I have been practicing for the last 20 years. Nevertheless, I think the second approach provides a clearer path for the security executive than the first one. None is absolutely perfect and you may have developed, through years of experience or strong thinking, another approach that fits the purpose.

Whatever the chosen approach, the questions you need to ask yourself are:

1. What does this security function or process produce?
2. What actions serve this function?
3. Which component makes the process?
4. How are we going to measure the evolution of these components through time?
5. What results are expected?

From there you must determine the following:

- Identify each security function/process the department is providing (e.g., access control, patrolling, policies and procedures, travel security).
- Determine what *drives* that function/process (is it labor, policies, systems-driven, etc.?). Why does it exist and how is it justified? Develop diagrams to show how the process works.
- Determine what can be measured (e.g., in the case of access to the office in the morning, one can easily measure the number of people arriving at work, number of cars, number of attempts at forced entries [tailgating], how many badges or office keys were forgotten on a specific date, how many cars are unlawfully parked [wrong parking, no windscreen sticker], etc.).
- Establish a data collection process (who will collect the data: patrol officers, dedicated security office, shift supervisor, etc.) and where it will be reported (Excel sheet, specific software, etc.).

- Determine what the data will depict and explain.
- Determine how the information will be illustrated (volume, trends, occurrences, percentage) depending on how best to describe the purpose behind the chosen metric and how it will be communicated to your management: weekly report, monthly report, annual report, and so on.
- Prioritize! This is of course paramount since you are preparing these metrics as part of strategic planning. What matters is to show your hierarchy that you work strategically and that you get results. You must always find an equilibrium between this idea of getting quick results and that of tackling what really matters to the management. Sometimes these items overlap, sometimes they do not. It might be unwise to focus on something the management wants if tangible results will not be seen before 18 months, for example. You must spread out your strategic long-term plan, with small tactical victories that will be seen by all.

CASE STUDY: CREATING A SIMPLE SECURITY INCIDENT REPORT

To create metrics, you need data. How you can get these data has been explained above and what follows is a simple illustration of the way you can organize yourself to be able to get material that you can exploit. What follows is derived from a simple security incident report I created and implemented during one of my stints of employment as security director in the Middle East, quite some time ago. What you see is a partial report, but it should be good enough to give you an idea of the principle to apply. It does not require high IT skills. It fits into an Excel sheet, so it permits all the presentations generously provided by the software—pies, columns, volumes, and so on. In this example, four security managers, quite distant from each other, report to you. Two are working on industrial sites (let us call them Factory 1 and Factory 2) and two are responsible for the security of headquarters in different cities (let us call them HQ1 and HQ2).

Each security manager has, on top of daily reports, a questionnaire to complete and send at the end of each month. The example focuses on access control and physical security and you are welcome to expand it to suit your own situation. But never overdo it and keep it simple. You might get lost in self-inflicted obstacles and fail to convince anybody, if your report is not easy to compile and difficult to read (Table 4.2).

115

Table 4.2 An Example of a Monthly Security Report

Monthly Security Activity Report

Location	Report drafted by	Position
Date of Report	Report approved by	Position

Access Control		Access Control Violations
Number of visitors	Employees	Visitors unescorted
	Visitors	Badge violations
	Contractors	Material ingress w/o permit
	VIPs	Documentation unauthorized
		Introduction of laptop/mobile phones
		Other forbidden items
Total entries		
Number of vehicles	Employees	Cars parked wrong spot
	Contractors	Cars parked in attributed spots
	Visitors	Cars parked w/o VIS
Total entries		

Physical Security	Physical Security Incidents
Number of patrols	Perimeter incidents
Number of rules violations	Suspicious vehicles at the periphery
Number of incidents	Suspicious activities
	Suspicious packages
	Parking incidents
	Material incidents
	Offices unlocked

Employee/Personnel Security	Employee/Personnel Security Incident
Number of employees on site	Suspicious behavior
Number of contactors	Workplace violence
	Theft
	Office negligence

The table is divided in two parts. On the left are the figures showing the reference numbers (people, cars, patrols, etc.—they are the referent data from which ratios and percentages will be calculated). On the right incidents are recorded. The combination of the incidents related to the referent (number of incidents proportional to the number of actions) makes the system very flexible, and some significant information can be obtained that way.

For example, the number of visitors found roaming the corridors unaccompanied may be measured against the number of people visiting the place during a specific month. 800 visitors and 2 unescorted visitors do not give the same image as 145 visitors and 15 found unescorted by security personnel. Another example, while we are at physical security, is that the number of cars parked in someone else's spot has value, particularly if the culprit is a permanent employee and a recidivist. For an employee, the path to good conduct follows the pattern of information (reminder of the policy), reinforced surveillance (CCTV surveillance and patrolling by security officers), warning, and eventually sanction.

THE RELIABILITY OF DATA

To be significant, the data collected and used in the security report need to be accurate. Information entered MUST reflect the reality of what happens and not what should happen in the field. When a post-order say that two patrols must be carried out during the day and two at night at a minimum, one can never be sure that the four patrols mentioned in the box "number of patrols" have really been carried out. Not because the officers did not want to do them, but perhaps because more important tasks have kept them busy. Patrols are often the first victims of a busy schedule. In that case, one could be tempted to fill in the forms as if the patrols had really happened to avoid having to justify the absence. This behavior must be fought, as it will lead to misleading results that could affect your overall strategy. The whole security hierarchy on site must be consistently reminded about the necessity of truthful reports. Patrols must be recorded, if possible, with a guard tour system or equivalent. I am a big fan of the guard tour system. It puts everyone's mind at rest and guarantees—to a certain extent—that the security officers were there, and it also tells you when they were there.

The reliability of figures is crucial to the conclusions you want to bring to the attention of the upper management.

117

An Excel sheet report lends itself easily to meaningful representations, such as chart, pie, and column presentations in order to identify trends, and the capabilities of Excel should be used to serve your purpose.

MULTIPLE SITES

If you are in charge of several sites, you can compile the data of all the sites and create a global report for the executive management. Tables and charts are good support for a monthly security report, emphasizing activities, but more importantly highlighting trends and security concerns. Be aware that differences in figures from one site to another may generate questions from the management. Get the answers ready.

More importantly, be concise and make your report as short as possible. Do not expect the top people to read a fifteen-page document each month. They simply do not have time for this and they will think that you do not have a synthetic mind and are not ready for moving up the corporate ladder.

To keep yourself at a strategic level, collate all the tables every month, keep them for your archives, and create a two-page report for the management: one page of writing, and one page of illustrations. Choose one issue per month, may be two, but not more. Select them on the basis of what we said earlier in this chapter. You must prioritize, always.

Then think about carefully maintaining these data because they will form the basis of your metrics.

After a first year of activity, you will be able to create a KPI that says, for example, To reduce the number of unescorted visitors in the HQ from 8% in Year X to a maximum of 2% by 31 December Year Y.

An advantage of compiling several sites' data and making a unique report is that it will help you evaluate the level and dedication of your different teams. No-incident reports a bit too frequently should alert you. Maybe the patrolling is not being carried out the way it should be (think *guard tour system*!), maybe the security officers do not do their job properly either by lack of motivation or by lack of training, or maybe morale is low for reasons you need to discover. Any no-incident report should trigger a reaction from your side and a visit to this crime-free paradise placed under your responsibility. This friendly visit, in my experience, is often enough to reverse the trend and instill some renewed dynamism in the team. This is also one of the reasons you should keep your compiled monthly reports with you and not make them available for all to see.

In one of my assignments, I had several security managers reporting to me. One ex-colonel, a man of integrity and dedication, sent reports that I thought were perfect. There were incidents, there were discoveries, and many of these discoveries had an impact on the well-being of the company (the discovery of water leaks during night patrol is one example). I had complete confidence in his ability both as a security practitioner and as a team leader. His people worked well because he knew how to get the best out of them. On another industrial site, located in another country, the security manager did not give me a good feeling from day one. He was a man of the verb, meaning that he answered yes to all my questions but could never show any supporting proof. When the first monthly report reached me, it confirmed my feelings. There had been no incidents whatsoever under his watch for a full month! I knew that taking a plane to ask for explanations was a complete waste of time, and Skype was not then what it is now. Anyway, I decided to observe first, giving the man the benefit of the doubt. So, for 3 months, I sent monthly reports to the top management with one of the sites displaying no-incident figures. It was an embarrassing situation and I was still trying to find a solution to it when one day I was visiting the GM on another matter of business, and he started discussing my report. What he said to me left me speechless. He told me that he was not very happy with the former colonel because obviously there were too many incidents on his watch, meaning he was not very good as a security manager. On the contrary, the man at Factory 2 was probably a top security manager since he managed to have no security incidents at all every month and should probably be promoted! Such an interpretation of figures had never crossed my mind and I was too taken aback to answer. But this was a good lesson.

Do not give figures to people of responsibility who know nothing about security. These figures are available to help you and not to harm your actions. I guess that some top managers apply the HSE principle that everything that tends toward zero is good. In security, it is not bad. There are security incidents all the time—there should be, and they should trigger reactions.

SUMMARY

Highlighting the performance of your security program will empower you with the capacity to see how it performs, *provided you chose the right indicators*. Measuring the number of cars poorly parked after hours in a far-off parking lot may not be valued information for your management. *Indicators must be relevant*. The measurements must tell a story, the story of the organization and the story of the impact of the security department on the integrity of the assets of the organization. Depending on what your company produces, the same indicator may have a very different value. Think thoroughly about which indicators can *answer questions to security problems*. Think about what the company is doing, what its assets are—tangible and intangible—what is of essential value to it (it can be pieces of equipment, plants, heavy machinery, a fleet of trucks, but it can also manuscripts, CDs, contracts, or maybe simply a unique recipe or individuals), and return to the mitigation measures that were recommended during the initial risk assessment of the organization. (This risk assessment should have been performed when you took over as security manager).

From there, use some kind of metric measurement system, for obvious reasons: (1) to be able to answer the questions from the management in quantitative terms, (2) to be able to measure your department's progress, and (3) to ensure that security is moving in the right direction.

This metric management system, or program, should be conceived as a very simple thing to start with. Select a few indicators that make common sense; then train your staff to be able to report—no, it is not obvious to report properly—and see how it works. If it works fine, then that's great. If recurrent incidents cannot find their place in your metrics matrix, modify the matrix to integrate the new indicators. Fine-tune your matrix during the first 3 to 6 months. Use graphics but only to a certain extent, keep the document short and colorful, and keep track of it in order to provide significant curves at the end of the year. By doing so, you will add value and the security department will be perceived as being both professional and proactive. Furthermore, never forget that the purpose of metrics management is to indicate trends and to warn of impeding unwanted security events. A gut feeling of being observed, tested, is fine, but the statistical proof that recent events may have been mock penetrations, attempts to locate the CEO offices, to observe the guards' change of shifts, is different. It gives weight to your analysis, makes your department valuable, and enhances your professional credibility.

Once your security program is implemented, you need to measure its effectiveness.

To do this, you will use security metrics. Security metrics are either hard (actions, events that can be counted) or soft (the example given is the effect of training of the competence of the guard force).

Security metrics allow the security manager to be more quantitative in his approach, a language management understands, but metrics can also show trends—in security breaches, for example—and justify changes in the security program based on these trends.

Metrics do not need to be complicated to be effective.

MAIN POINTS

- Remember that what gets measured gets done!
- Only business-significant items should be considered.
- Take the viewpoint of management when selecting metrics.
- Beware of the temptation to measure only what can be counted! Feelings and perceptions do count and can be measured.
- There is more to KPIs than KPIs: Understand critical success factors and select key result areas.
- Create a simple metrics measurement system that can provide meaningful security statistics to the management.
- Make your reports concise and to the point, and rely on them to justify your demands!

END NOTE

[1] A metric is defined as a standard of measurement using quantitative, statistical, and/or mathematical analysis.

REFERENCES

Campbell, G. K. (2007) *Measures and Metrics in Corporate Security: Communicating Business Value*. Security Executive Council: Framingham, MA.

Cole, R. B. (2003) *Measuring Security Performance & Security*. ASIS International: Alexandria, VA.

Dobbins, R. and Pettman, B.O. (2006) 3rd ed. *What Self-Made Millionaires Really Think, Know and Do: A Straight-Taking Guide to Business Success and Personal Riches*. Capstone Publishers: Chichester, UK.

Doss, K. T. (2011) 2nd ed. *PSP Study Guide*. ASIS International: Alexandria, VA.

Kovacich, G. L. & Halibozek, E. P. (2006) *Security Metrics Management: How to Manage the Costs of an Assets Protection Program*. Butterworth-Heinemann: Amsterdam, the Netherlands.

Perois, J. (2016) *Getting the First Step Right: A Risk Assessment Guide for The Security Manager*. ASIS International: Alexandria, VA.

5

Maintaining the Security Program
Awareness, Training, and Audits

INTRODUCTION

Some readers may wonder how maintenance is relevant. Chapter 4 emphasized the need to measure your security program to make it significant. Time will tell, in the eyes of the management at least, whether your clever strategic security plan has had any positive impact on the security posture of the organization and the integrity of its assets and operations. One often sees a new security manager implement important changes during their first year of tenure, after which they appear to sit back and relax while the new program falls into a routine followed not long afterward by the return of bad habits.

Even if the management has welcomed your enthusiasm, they are still a bit worried about your security strategic plan and probably remain to be convinced of its necessity (on the basis of the *it did not exist before and we never had an incident* principle, probably the most difficult opinion to overcome in our profession). As long as costs are not involved, you will not feel major reluctance at your demeanor and determination. You need to give your management time to grasp what you are doing. You may be the first security director who is not happy with simply running a guard force, checking parking lots, and running a badging workshop, but who is willing to instill a genuine security attitude in the business. After all, you can spend a full career doing what some call solid security, and give entire satisfaction to your management.

Whatever your program, avoid pretending that your approach is strategic! Strategy, or so the management believes, is not something a security manager should be preoccupied with. Just mention changing times, evolving best practices, and the need to benchmark favorably with the competition. This usually does the trick! Give them time to get used to your ideas and objectives. Once the top brass understand that they can benefit from your new master plan, things will go much smoother. It is often imperceptible, but you will feel it.

Having the top management accepting you as part of the operational process will already be a major victory. If you manage to sit at the weekly meeting with the other managers and VPs, consider it an achievement!

Be that as it may, this should not prevent you from thinking strategically about your department and its place in the organization. Behave as if you were part of the strategic plan, because, your supervisors may not know it, but you are. And therefore, apply the principles that you would apply if you were the chief security officer of a multinational corporation.

And one principle you must stick to during your career is to make sure that your security program is maintained in a substantial way.

The purpose in this chapter is to establish a link between the overall strategy of the security department and the different forms of the maintenance program.

This maintenance program can take many forms and be served by very different activities, but its most common are:

> security briefings, videos, the dissemination of desktop instructional materials, formal training in specific security subject areas, posters, flyers, the use of daily or weekly bulletins, and any other possible ideas that will assist you in instilling a positive view and support of your fellow employees for the overall security program. (Roper et al. 2006: 37)

SECURITY AWARENESS AS PART OF THE MAINTENANCE PROGRAM

The security awareness program is the perfect tool to: (1) make your security program known to the workforce, (2) widen the scope of security while gaining adhesion and creating a bond with the employees, and (3) keep the security program alive and pertinent.

The security awareness program, whatever the topics covered, belongs to the domain of administrative security. Indeed, once the administrative elements of the program—policies, plans, procedures, post-orders—are in place, those who are expected to comply with or implement them need to (1) be aware of their existence, (2) know what these policies and procedures consist of, and (3) understand (and endorse the idea) of how one should act to become an active (and even sometime proactive) part of this asset protection program. Awareness is a permanent feature of a maintenance program and any change in the security master plan should generate some security awareness actions.

The strategic purpose behind security awareness, though, is not to make the policies known. This could be done through any communication means sent to the staff (email, intranet, memorandum, distributed booklet). Strategically, it is about gaining support from the employees, making them part of the security team, like some sort of honorary security wardens, while promoting the idea that a well-protected company is a better place to work. This chapter will not teach you how to build a security awareness program. There are books on this topic and they provide excellent guidelines and advice to succeed.

Our purpose is rather to think about how to best serve your interests—remember, you must always come first—and those of the security department. You have, in fact, huge leeway to organize your security awareness sessions. See them as one of the most important elements of your maintenance program and one you can entirely drive and direct in any direction you want. If you are interested in widening your knowledge of awareness, I will suggest that you refer to Roper et al. (2006), which is the best book on security awareness I have read. In 2007, I used it to prepare a complete security awareness program, and although it was not fully implemented for a lot of reasons that had little to do with security but much with internal politics, it met, at its conception, no criticism from my hierarchy. Everything in Roper's book is there to help you create a solid and well-conceived security awareness program. For now, I will give a small summary of what can be done and highlight how it interacts with the maintenance program and how it supports the strategic plan.

The Audience/Target People and Their Specific Needs

You have great latitude in terms of audience and of course it will depend on what your organization produces. In headquarters, there will be senior and/or middle managers, but also secretaries, while in a facility there will be admin and operations people, several layers of them in each case. Whatever their responsibilities in the organization, they need to receive some common training as well as some specific training. As a matter of fact, the whole workforce should benefit from awareness sessions, from the CEO down to the most basic employees, whatever their roles may be. The entire staff can be subject to identical threats. Social engineering comes immediately to mind, meaning that social engineering could become a topic for a short presentation open to all. Moreover, each employee in their own field of operations could be subject to specific threats. Contract departments, HR, research and development, secretaries, operators, and so on will face different threats, and your job will be to prepare security awareness sessions adapted to both common and specific threats.

As an example, top managers could be facing the common threats in addition to specific threats linked to their status in the organization (abduction, kidnapping, attempted murder, workplace violence), while people who travel a lot face threats that should be dealt with during travel security awareness sessions. All this is common sense, and you and your team should think in generic terms as well as consider specific populations and the threats they might face. The result, generic and specific security awareness sessions, if well conceived and delivered, will be received positively. The fact that certain at-risk populations have a program to especially address their security needs usually buys their support. It is therefore up to you to present a diversified security awareness program using the tools at your disposal and covering the broadest spectrum of the workforce, as well as generic sessions that could be enjoyed by all and will create rapport between you and the workforce and generate a feeling of belonging.

Your imagination (and your budget) are the limits to what can be done in terms of awareness, but traditional tools are briefings, booklets, presentations, and poster campaigns.

BRIEFINGS

A good start would be to make sure that a (short) security briefing is integrated into the induction program for all new employees. If possible, have one of your staff present during these inductions and have your own slides (the initial induction session is often delivered via PowerPoint by HR people). Insist on having a few slides about security in the presentation and if possible send one of your most pleasant security officers to attend, answer questions, and give a friendly human face to security. I worked once for a company where the charming women in charge of the induction program just jumped the existing security slides because they found them "uninteresting" and "embarrassing"—something I discovered during my own induction session. It was a nice welcome and an eye-opener about the perception of security in the company. I knew I had some serious work ahead of me! Now, if you work on an industrial site, there is always a safety briefing for each person entering the operations area. Insist on bringing some security elements into this type of briefing (badge wearing, visitors accompanied at all times, prohibition on taking photos, etc.). During one of my trips to South Korea, I noticed that in industrial complexes, mobile phones were not prohibited—as they often are in the Middle East—but stickers were put on the camera of the phone. Stickers that, once taken away, would not stick anymore! A simple inspection of your mobile phone before they returned your passport was all security needed to know if you had been indulging in a bit of industrial espionage.

Roper et al. suggest that there should be at least four basic-level presentations within the employee's life cycle: (1) the initial (welcome to the company), (2) a refresher (annual update and reminders), (3) travel briefings (inside and outside the country), and (4) termination (discharge, retirement, transfer, etc.) (Roper et al. 2006: 42).

Employees should also attend security training according to their responsibilities and the level of confidential information they are entrusted with. HR people, for example, would traditionally be the target of social engineering (internally, for example, to inquire about the salary and perks of a colleague, and externally, for probably the same reasons and possibly more ominous ones). Those in the company who travel abroad often carry with them trade secrets, draft business agreements, or technical data that should not fall into the hands of adversaries or competitors. They need to be made aware of the threats and of the role they have to play in protecting the organization's confidential data, and they must learn about the different ways to thwart or at least divert the threats without putting their life at risk. The list of potential awareness topics is quite extensive. All employees need to be regularly briefed.

Security for Visitors

I understand that the issues of security briefings for visitors is a not an easy one. You cannot send someone from security to do a security briefing for every visitor that enters the facility or the office tower. It would be impractical and slightly ridiculous (unless you work for a nuclear plant or an intelligence agency). I have seen two ways of dealing with this. One is to add a few bullet points on the safety briefing which everybody seems to find perfectly natural (my guess is that the safety people in charge will, at best, read the bullet points, although apologetically). Another option is to have a small pamphlet printed that visitors receive once they have signed the visitor book and been given their visitor's badge. The visitor would sign for both entering the place and having received the security induction brochure. In my many visits to many places, I never really met the perfect solution for visitors. Using a visitor management program, briefing your guard force properly, and sensitizing the employees to such issues as visitor management is the best one can do.

BOOKLETS OR ONLINE INFORMATION

By booklets, I mean guides, pamphlets, or any other piece of paper you can use to promote your security program for an internal purpose. A security fact of the week on the intranet also falls into this category. Each briefing should be coupled with a paper illustration that will be given to the employees at events such as the security induction program and the security and safety briefing. PowerPoint presentations should be accompanied by a colored sheet with important facts to remember. However, make sure before you print anything that your company (i.e., your management) approves of it. As a matter of fact, most companies are very strict about any publications bearing their logo. For obvious reasons (image, liability), they want to keep control over all company documents. Do not be surprised if you are faced with a long compliance list and a lot of check-ups before your publications, as trivial and benign as they may appear to you, are approved.

The purpose of online information is mainly to remind everyone that you are there and that security consists of more important things than checking badges and closing offices left open at night. You must instill, slowly but steadily, the idea that the workplace is not as insignificant as most employees think it is and that its security should not be taken for granted. Whatever your company produces, there are adversaries, competitors, and people who would like it not to succeed. Put in the workforce's mind that a well-protected company is an organization that grows and creates (or at least maintains) employment. Too often in my life I have seen people taking the workplace for granted, never thinking about what it does, how it survives, how it makes a profit, and ultimately how it pays them. This spirit must be changed and you, as an executive, should contribute to this change.

SECURITY AWARENESS PRESENTATIONS

Depending on the atmosphere in your company and the perception of the security department by the top management, you may try to offer security awareness presentations once a month or once a term on generic and specific security topics. This is something I never achieved in my short corporate life and one of my regrets. As a consultant, though, I have been asked to build security awareness programs for the workforce with relative success and I ignore whether these awareness sessions were delivered or not. So, my recommendations here are purely theoretical. But I put a lot of thought and efforts into preparing security awareness programs for big organizations and have a good idea of the complexity of doing so as well as of the difficulty of implementing such programs. Presenting a 30-minute PowerPoint on—let us keep the same example—social engineering and industrial espionage requires a tremendous amount of work. One must gather interesting facts and tangible examples, bring the information to the level of the audience, find good quality illustrations, and condense it all into a 12-slide-maximum presentation, keeping 10 minutes for questions.

This is the first difficulty. The second is to have your presentation approved for the reasons mentioned earlier. You run the risk of seeing your management falling suddenly victim to a bout of *Polyanna* syndrome,[1] and abruptly declaring that your awareness session is a complete waste of time.

The third, and not the least, difficulty is to attract people to your presentation. It is not just making them come to your place. It is rather making their line managers send them to your talk. Without the support of the line supervisors, your chances of success are virtually non-existent. There are several ways to approach these line managers and none are easy or simple. First, you must ensure that the top management support your initiative. By top management, I mean really the top authority, because on security issues, people belonging to the inner circle rarely agree. So, get the CEO (or GM, whoever runs the show) to approve your presentation program. Then, if you belong to the management weekly meeting, just inform your peers, in front of the CEO, who, with some luck, may officially support the initiative. Then, speak individually to the main managers, whenever you can, to familiarize them with the issue and make sure that they will not object to letting their people spend 30 minutes away from their workstations. Then, eventually, communicate the dates and location of the presentation, via the intranet, when you have one, through grouped emails if you do not. Ask people to commit to the meeting. You need to book a room and get some croissants—or any healthy alternative—in the room along with coffee and tea.

There is no guarantee the course will be successful, and I would lying if I told you that this is the recipe for successful awareness presentations. But again, I think it is worth a try. I think that anything that de-dramatizes security and makes it closer to the employees goes in the right direction and should be encouraged. Your goal, as a strategist, is to break the image of the corporate cop, because people picture you in a bad light. They perceive the police as a repressive entity: *cop image = punishment*. You want to convey the image of corporate security as that of a protector and an enabler: *corporate security = enabler and protector*. There is a long away to go except if your predecessor has already worked hard in that direction. If that is the case, discuss it with your security cadres to establish a program to take from where she left to where you want to go.

Another item that we security professionals are quite reluctant to admit to is the generally low credibility of security people. As Roper aptly says, "The callous watchdog style of so many security officials in years past, unfortunately, has poisoned the air for many firms and agencies"

(Roper et al. 2006: 91). You may have some of these dinosaurs on your own staff, and they must be converted or at least neutralized. The success of your awareness program depends enormously upon the credibility of you and your people.

Internal Obstacles

On your team, you may have all sorts of people, with different backgrounds and sensitivities. Some of them will find your project exhilarating, while others will find it a complete waste of time. You must accept the diversity of your guard force because it is a given. You will have ex-cop, ex-military, ex-shopping mall guards, and even some people that never really were in law enforcement at all, and embraced the profession by pure chance. These people see the world differently and might resent what they perceive as a threat to the little authority they have. You have to work on them first. You must demonstrate without being demagogic what's in it for each member of your team. Security officers might have difficulty understanding that while they try to instill some respect for the rules in the organization, their boss is playing Mr. Nice Guy, working hard to seduce what they see as undisciplined employees. You will have to explain your plan and strategy to the security guard force to make sure that you're all reading from the same sheet. The security officers, used to harboring an unquestioned authority for most of their professional life, may think that playing security differently will take power away from them. You will need some solid pedagogy to tell them that you do not want to reduce their authority, but only "rechannel" it in a friendlier, but also more effective, direction by getting the workforce to become part of the whole security program. I cannot promise it will be easy. What you must do is work very hard on the *what's in it for me* for the security officers. See your program from their perspective and try to find out how they will benefit: skills? knowledge? image? prestige? specific training? promotion? etc. In the same way that you customize the security program to specific employee groups, you must customize a security program for the security guard force.

A security awareness program works on several levels. The first one, dedicated to the guard force itself, must be well conceived if you want it to be well received. Like all awareness programs, it must perform a number of functions—"advise, indoctrinate, familiarize, inform and instruct" (Roper et al. 2006: 39)—but it must also work on the psychological mechanisms of the security officers. It must convince the doubtful that security is moving in the right direction, but wants to take the rest of the workforce in its swing. It is not simple and needs some thinking. Of course, this change should be reflected in your personal attitude toward the workforce and the guard force. You should demonstrate through your daily behavior that your security employees are your partners and not solely your subordinates. Reaching the right balance is difficult, particularly when cultural difference may lead your attitude to be misinterpreted.

Remember that culture dictates, and if you work with a multicultural workforce you must do like the Romans do. For those of us who served in the military with some level of responsibility (commissioned or non-commissioned officers) the issue should not be new, and we had ample time to reflect on ways to inspire subordinates, as well as to create enthusiasm and motivate while still being obeyed. For readers who embraced security as a first career and went from university to the industry without passing by the khaki garment, these things might be more difficult to apprehend. There are skills involved in commanding, and I am not sure that universities prepare young men and women to manage men and women, particularly older men. Business schools might be more involved in the issue, but I did not graduate from any of them and I ignore what they teach. There is also an innate part to commanding, and not all of us are bestowed with that gift. I have friends who made a full career in the military and who nevertheless never found the right balance in their style of command. This did not prevent them from reaching acceptable ranks. This is perhaps more an art than anything else, and some do it naturally (which is all the more irritating for those who try their best with lesser results), but after all, this is the rule for all social interactions.

The second awareness program must be prepared for your management. You will have to box very cleverly and prepare an answer to all the questions that will inevitably be fired at you: How much will that cost? What time will be taken from real work? What will be the return on investment? This last question is obviously the most important question that will be asked in the end, and in passing. In reality, this is all that counts. This is why you must prepare your program and choose your examples with great care. It may seem obvious that an awareness training program about preventing kidnapping and abduction for executives deployed in areas where kidnapping is the favorite sport makes very much sense for a company that has already paid hefty ransoms to get their employees back. Including the families within this awareness program will usually be seen positively, for the very same reasons. Partners and children are more likely to be kidnapped than employees working in an office most of the time. Here the return on investment (ROI) is quite obvious and provided you are reasonable in your cost estimate, it should meet with little to no resistance. The same goes for travel awareness. It is a bitter pill to swallow when you start working on the basics, clean desk policies, parking lot, access control, CPTED suggestions, and so on. In fact, everything that is not linked to an increase in production will not be seen with sympathy. Avoiding piggybacking or tailgating will not pique anyone's interest, unless you can prove or suggest strongly that not working on it costs money. When I was 16 and 17, I worked during summer holidays in a Parisian bank. This was a massive bank and I worked at the clearing house, counting checks from other banks that would have to be exchanged later. As you can guess, still in high school, I was very naïve regarding the work habits (ethics?) of older people, but I remember one thing that really stunned me, to say the least. At lunchtime, every employee had to log out, and then back in. Everybody knows that lunchtime for French people is an important thing, much more than for people in English-speaking countries, but I observed that after lunch, one guy carried all the access cards from the rest of the team, so the others could stay at the pub and play games and drink beers. Half an hour or sometimes even an hour later, the rest of the group came back, going through the gate with the complicity of one of the security officers. It was a daily routine for those guys who considered that they were both underpaid and undervalued. This is not something I want to discuss now, but putting an end to that scam would have been seen as a good reason for doing an awareness program about it. Whether it would have convinced other employees to denounce such unacceptable behavior is far from certain, but fixing the access control issue, making all employees aware of the unacceptable behaviors of some elements, and getting rid of disloyal security officers would have justified the program.

Make sure that you can provide convincing examples when you submit your program to your immediate supervisor or it will stay on her desk forever.

When you have jumped over all these hurdles, the job is not done—far from it. You may think that convening employees around coffee and croissants to discuss issues of general interest, such as phishing or social engineering, cannot fail and that your room will be full and the audience enthused. You did everything right, or so you think. You chose Monday morning to show the management—among them the supervisors who allowed their employees to participate—that you do not intend to waste working time. You chose a simple and sufficiently generic topic to avoid controversy and the irritation of your peers, but this does not guarantee that your enthusiasm will be mirrored. If only a few brave persons show up, do not be disappointed. You need to tame people, and this takes time.

During this first session, start establishing unwritten rules, like the way you arrange chairs, who from the security department will attend, whether you will have croissants or donuts accompanying coffee and tea, whether you will choose a PowerPoint presentation followed by questions and answers or use an open discussion with tables arranged in circle, and so on. You will see quite quickly what works and what does not. You will progress probably through trial and error. I have read somewhere that it is a good idea in such instances to loosen your tie down and look relaxed (an image U.S. presidents seem to enjoy and that has been imitated by most Western heads of state and other governments), but I am not sure that you should look different from how you do every day. Your audience will not fall for that. They will see through this tactic immediately and feel that the purpose of the meeting is to manipulate them, which is never a good start. Just be yourself; you are a security professional after all, it shows, and people understand that you have responsibilities and accept that. They just do not like to have their freedom impinged upon, and you should also understand that (this does not mean you have to accept it, though). Try to make your presentations alive with examples, give them something to remember that can be taken back home. It is not that complicated, and it will enhance the image of the security department. If it goes well, you will end up seeing the supervisors attending—they also want some interesting information coming their way—and eventually some line managers.

A SECURITY AWARENESS POSTER CAMPAIGN

I worked on my first security poster campaign around 15 years ago in the GCC. The QHSE & S department (quality, health, safety, environment and security, quite a portfolio!) vice president had decided on a new safety campaign and I used this opportunity to suggest having a security poster campaign at the same time. He initially thought it was a good idea and feeling supported, I embraced the project with gusto. There had never been a security campaign since the company began operating, and my VP agreed that it would be worth a try, provided security adopted a rather low profile in this exercise. Not being in a position to enforce or impose anything, I could only agree with my superior and tried my best to reach a balance between efficiency and discretion.

Such an apparently minor campaign revealed that a lot of work was necessary. Simple posters above photocopy machines, above shredders, and in the hall to make sure that all employees wear badges is a very stimulating endeavor, but it seems that only security people really get excited about it. I worked for several months on such a campaign, only to have my campaign just canceled by the CEO at the last minute because he thought that doing a security campaign could send the signal to competitors, neighbors, and employees that we had serious security issues in the company, while of course safety campaigns were regularly updated and seemed to benefit from an almost unlimited budget! My main mistake in this endeavor, and the one I shared with my immediate supervisor, was to have overlooked the cultural aspects of the campaign. A few months of effort was reduced to nil by misunderstanding, or at least overlooking, different cultural perceptions. Why do we always have to learn the hard way?

NEGLECTING THE CULTURAL ASPECT: THE ULTIMATE MISTAKE

In Saudi Arabia in the early 2000s, I was in charge of a group of expatriate workers deployed in Jeddah on a big co-operation project that was responsible for the security and well-being of thirty expatriates, plus a number of people deployed for short period of times to provide specific technical duties.

This population was very homogenous in terms of background, and following an attack in Karachi (Pakistan), the company that employed my company wanted to make sure that no misadventures would happen to their team working in Saudi Arabia. My task, among many others, consisted mainly in baby-sitting the workforce, who were simply not convinced of the reality of the threat! Believe me, in 2004–2005 years, the threat for Western expatriates in Saudi Arabia was very real. People deployed in the country were sent as bachelors. They were split between two compounds that really provided sufficient sports facilities in very comfortable flats, with a level of comfort far superior to what these people would have enjoyed in Europe in comparable circumstances (although none admitted it, of course). All spoke the same language and shared the same culture. They intended to survive their mission and accepted the job with money as a solid motivator. This made our task (I had a colleague with me) quite easy. It was also quite easy to gather them in one of the compounds for an awareness session about the threat and the ways to remain vigilant without ceding to panic. This homogenous human material coupled with their isolation in an Arabic-/English-speaking country made them more receptive to our security discourse. The only people who objected to this approach was the overseas management personnel who feared that if they were scared beyond reason, workers would break their contract and demand an immediate return to France (or demand unreasonable risk premiums). There was an equilibrium to find between providing too much information, and risk spooking the workers, and not enough, giving them the feeling of wasting their time.

During my tenure as a corporate advisor a few years later in the UAE, I had to face a situation with two major differences. First, the threat in the UAE was perceived as almost negligible, and second, the company I worked for had perhaps as many nationalities working for it as there are countries registered at the United Nations (a slight exaggeration, I admit). This cultural diversity was relatively manageable. All what most expatriate employees wanted was to get on with their work that provided the sole income of their families abroad. As a consequence, security was fairly well accepted by them, although it was not taken very seriously. Suicide bombers in Abu Dhabi were not a daily occurrence... No, the real issue, for me, was the management.

When I was under U.S. management during the first 2 years of my tenure, I was thinking on par with the top management and almost all my suggestions were endorsed. When the project became operations and that management passed into local hands, things changed drastically! The local management disagreed entirely with my evaluation of the threat. For them there was no threat whatsoever...and so far, they have been proved right; no attack has occurred either to the plant or to the HQ since I left. This is a good illustration of cultural diversity. While Westerners perceived the whole region as frought with danger, local management was convinced that security issues were non-existent. They equated security with terrorism, and since terrorism was dealt with at the government level, they saw no point in having a strong security posture. A few shopping mall guards in uniforms to open doors and sometime provide valet parking would perfectly do the job. I must admit that none of the Westerners on my team saw the change in direction coming. But when the new GM arrived, I did a presentation to explain what we were doing, why we were doing it, and how we were doing it. At the end of the presentation, the GM asked a few questions, visibly uninterested by the topic, and when he left the room, I said to the colleague standing next to me, "In 1 year, we are all gone." And that is more or less the time it took to get rid of all the expatriates in the department. Not that we were right and they were wrong, not even the opposite; simply put, our cultural predispositions were different and our perspectives irreconcilable.

The same misadventure could happen to the maintenance of your security program. Whatever the reasons behind the decisions, the cultural aspect will prevail. If your proposal offends the local culture, or the intercultural relations in the organization, it will not be allowed. It would be better to test the water early to avoid serious disappointment.

When you propose your campaign, make sure that its spirit is not aggressive. There are many security awareness organizations that sell amusing and entertaining posters online, which can be customized with your company logo and colors. Present your campaign with a light tone, and make it universal. In the GCC, for example, I have noticed that safety poster campaigns where mistakes are described always portray a Westerner making the mistakes. It would be considered inappropriate to show local people falling asleep at the wheel or doing anything else bad. A Western model is always employed to show the "don't." This is a fact of life linked to cultural perceptions of self. Be aware of them, and ask for advice before you launch yourself into a complicated and dangerous campaign. I do not know why the spirit (or rather the excuse) of confidentiality reigns supreme in regards to security while safety is free to advertise almost anything they want. There is definitely a wrong attitude about security as if their contents were secret and should not be shared (while they are policies and procedures emanating from and approved by the top management!), though yes, I have seen efforts preventing the employees from knowing the security policies and procedures because they need to be kept confidential! Yes, you understood that correctly. A massive industrial facility paid my company a comfortable sum of money to write policies, plans, and procedures, which went through a lengthy approval process and ended up in the office of the plant security superintendent, never to be shared with anybody! This is an extreme case, of course, but it highlights the fact that talking about security might be sensitive.

Security needs to be well known in the organization, if we want it to become a dynamic function and you want it to serve your career plans. And to be fair, employees should become a major part of this function, because at the end of the day, it benefits them!

EMPOWERING YOUR GUARD FORCE:
TRAINING AS MAINTENANCE

Although training is an integral part of security "maintenance," we will keep this paragraph short since the topic has been considered earlier in this chapter. Keep in mind, though, that *training is the key to morale*. A regularly trained guard force is a guard force with strong self-confidence, and this in itself is a serious deterrent for any adversarial observer. This self-confidence shows in their attitude, their body language, and the neatness of their uniforms, and it will also generate respect from the rest of the employees. There are many courses available on the market, some of which are online, to improve skills and knowledge in your guard force. Some cost as little as a few dozen dollars. Some can be taken in your town. You can use the skills inside your team to build training programs. Kane has written a mastery book that says everything you need to know about security training and I recommend you buy this book, which contains everything you need to deliver sound and adequate training to any security guard force (Kane 2000). Remember that your officers are your ambassadors and that they reflect your commitment and enthusiasm.

What is important when it comes to training the guard force is that early in your assignment, you take the measure of the capabilities of your team members in terms of development and then prepare a career development program for each of them. All of them will not be able to replace you, but all should be allowed to progress through a motivating career, and for this they need to develop self-confidence. It is essential that they see themselves as competent, professional, and respected individuals. Remember that in many countries in the world, security officers are looked down on by the rest of the workforce and perceived as lazy and stupid. To reveal their existing potential and boost their self-esteem is a worthy task that will reflect positively on you as a manager. If you work for a big organization, you would be well advised to approach the human resources manager to discuss the possibility of promotion and advancement for the security workforce. I did it in one of my assignments and was only half surprised to learn that there was no development plan for the guard force at all. Too much turnover, I was told, and so easy to replace. Wrong and sad, but in many companies, it is an attitude that is fairly accepted.

I think that looking after your people and trying to give them a career is something you should strive for. It may not help you in your career, perhaps, but is personally and professionally rewarding. I have spent a long time in security and there are far more good apples than bad ones.

REGULAR UPDATES

Implementing your security program will take time, and once it is up and running, you are entitled to a bit of a rest. But do not relax for too long. Maintain at a minimum an annual review of your security program with submission of your report to the management. You want to show that security is a proactive/dynamic department, that you are a real manager, and you also want to keep your team on their toes. I think that a review of the security program, with your team first, followed by a presentation to the executive management, will put you in a good light. During this presentation, make sure that you emphasize the fact that everything there is meant to serve the strategic goals of the company, and that it is not just to keep yourself busy. Insist on having an annual presentation. Some of your superiors will think that you overrate your importance by this, and few managers want to hear about security, fearing bad news. But keep insisting on it. I did not when I was in the position to do so as a director of security, and I am sure it harmed my image. I was told the CEO was too busy, my VP said he knew what I was doing and did not need another presentation. I did not insist enough and in retrospect, I see now that I was wrong. Do not let yourself be pushed away from you what you think you should do. It will harm you in the end. Often, you will notice that insistence pays significant dividends.

If you manage to make your presentations interesting, you will see that the CEO appreciates an annual briefing, or sometimes even a twice yearly briefing. What matters is that this briefing will be one of the rare occasions where you will be facing her on a one-to-one basis. It will give you a hint of the current concerns of the management and also of the CEO as a person. Any such meeting should be food for thought. Your job is to serve your CEO the best you can and you must make sure that this is what you do when implementing your security program. By doing so repeatedly, you might be able to put the security department on the corporate map and yourself at the same time.

THE SECURITY AUDIT

The security audit is a must in every organization. Here, we call it a security audit (a security audit measures existing security against a standard); however, it can simply be called a security survey. A security survey is a survey during which existing security is measured against best practices.

If it is an audit, it is simple. Take the standard of reference—your company may have its own—and tick the boxes. If your company does not follow standards, you can either create your own or use one of the many available on the market. Floyd (2008), for example, proposes security survey templates for the following entities:

- Manufacturing plants
- Retails stores
- Distribution centers
- Office buildings
- Private residences
- Closed and abandoned facilities

His practical spiral-bound book is available from the ASIS International Bookstore (www.asisonline.org) and is sold with a CD that should really make your life easier. You can also find excellent surveys in Vellani (2007), Sennewald (2003), and Perois (2016).

SUMMARY AND THE IMPACT OF MAINTENANCE, AWARENESS, AND TRAINING ON YOUR OVERALL STRATEGY

A security maintenance program is a must in any serious security department. Its purpose is to keep the security posture of the organization at an acceptable level of preparedness. The terms of use should be straightforward and appear in the security master plan that the top management has already approved. Security maintenance is expected of you and your department and should reflect solid methods and realism, and it should interfere as little as possible with operations. The security maintenance program is what makes you a manager in the eyes of the C-suite, provided it is properly advertised. I often mention this motto that I heard in the military: *Do little, do it well, and above all, let it be known.* Putting yourself forward, in the corporate context, is a necessity and a skill that many of us never learned or felt comfortable with. You might fight this coyness and show yourself for what you are: a manager and an important one.

Building up a security awareness program is a touchy issue, full of traps, and must be approached with caution. In theory, it is also part of your brief, but reality says otherwise. In big multicultural organizations, it can even be a dangerous experience. Even from people you think are on your side, expect surprise, mistrust, antagonism, and a little bit of backstabbing.

Think long and hard before starting the process and if you decide to go for it, keep your objective basic and adopt a low profile. Stick to existing and approved policies (clean desk policy, information protection policy, etc.) and try to be generic and never point fingers at any specific members of the organization by genre, nationality, or religious affiliation. Security awareness must be soft and positive in tone, and it should not hurt feelings. That is rule number one. It must be funny, original, and discreet. That is rule number two. And rule number three is that it must be circumscribed to a limited period of time, because a long campaign loses its impact.

As demonstrated, training is another way to make sure that your guard force remains motivated and enthusiastic. Address training early in the process because it is often complicated to gain management approval in certain administrative structures. Think of your officers as employees entitled to a rewarding career, and support those who want to improve themselves. Looking out for your employees will have a beneficial strategic impact on the way you are perceived.

Keep the executive management aware of your deeds. Let them know that you are not static in your position, but that you want to improve what can be improved. Show innovation if you can, but always keep in mind that executives hate surprises and always have the answer to the "What will that cost?" question. When you try something new, use your network of midlevel management colleagues (HR, training, admin, IT, etc.) to test the waters. In other words, be flexible and ready to abandon unpopular ideas. Update your security program because strong security behaviors tend to weaken after a while. Discipline is a virtue that needs constant monitoring to be maintained at the right level. With time, employees tend to return to lax behaviors that should be discouraged. Through awareness, but also through observation, the workforce must be made aware that security is there and intends to maintain the high level of integrity and efficiency required to carry out the protection of the organization's assets.

SUMMARY

To sum up this chapter, let us state that, like all human endeavors, a security program needs maintenance. This maintenance is what will keep the program relevant, and therefore credible. This credibility will reflect on your image as a security practitioner and as a manager. The maintenance program will also help you understand what part of security has been improving and what kind of new trends are emerging. Threats do change, but so do behaviors, and a security program must evolve with these changing demands.

MAIN POINTS

- Although security awareness is a natural part of a maintenance program, it may be faced with particular resistance
  from the management.
- Briefing and inductions are part of the maintenance program.
  Fight your way into these existing and accepted programs.
- Have any security awareness program approved on principle
  even before you start working on it. Be very clear on what the
  program will entail and which messages it will convey.
- Be very attentive to the cultural perception of security
  awareness, particularly if you are deployed abroad, in a
  multicultural organization.
- Training is capital to the maintenance of a solid security
  program. Train your people, train employees, train your
  hierarchy, and train yourself.
- Regular security audits—or surveys—are the best way to
  show the relevance of the security program and the state of
  preparedness of your department.

END NOTE

[1] The Polyanna syndrome is characterized by the tendency to be unrealisti-
cally optimistic: It never happened here before, so why should we talk about
it and make it a problem now?

REFERENCES

Floyd, W. R. (2008) *Security Surveys*. ASIS International: Alexandria, VA.

Kane, P. (2000) *Practical Security Training*. Butterworth-Heinemann: Boston, MA.

Perois. J. (2016) *Getting the first step right: a risk assessment guide for the security
manager*. ASIS International: Alexandria, VA.

Roper, C. A., Grau, J. A., & Fischer, L. F. (2006) *Security Education, Awareness and
Training: From Theory to Practice*. Elsevier: Burlington, MA.

Sennewald, C. A. (2003) *Effective Security Management*. Butterworth-Heinemann:
Boston, MA.

Vellani, K. H. (2007) *Strategic Security Management: A Risk Assessment Guide for
Decision Makers*. Butterworth-Heinemann: Boston, MA.

6

Personal Strategy
A Crash Course in Self Development

WHY CREATING A GOOD PLAN MAY
NOT IMPROVE YOUR CAREER

Security Not Perceived as a Regalian Portfolio

Time and again I have observed that security managers, some of them remarkable individuals on all counts, are not rewarded for their efforts in the corporate environment. Security professionals seldom make it to the apex of an organization and the reasons for this are not simple. I have worked more as an external consultant than in corporate positions, but these few years around the Monday morning management meeting table left me with a quite disagreeable feeling. The feeling of not being esteemed, not only myself as a person but the security department as a whole, by the colleagues sitting around that table. But feelings may just be that: feelings. And to make sure that I was not victim of a deeply ingrained inferiority complex, I asked some fellow practitioners whether they shared this feeling or not. When I asked my friend and colleague Stephen Green, a British security engineer I have known for many years, what his thoughts were about this topic, he replied:

> That's a good question, and one which I have a personal interest in. On a daily basis, I see the wildly differing levels of respect afforded me, depending on whether I'm wearing my engineer's hat, or that of a security professional. Even though I am able to stand as a chartered

security professional alongside chartered engineers,[1] I am not treated as a peer. I believe that this comes down to simple familiarity. Office administration, finance, personnel, and even facilities management are all well-understood roles; they are often elements of MBA courses, so senior management talk the language of these functions. Few talk the language of security. Only those who work in industries existentially dependent on security (nuclear, defense, custodial services, etc.) understand the true value of it and have taken the effort to understand its basis and ethos. More commonly, companies employ security as a "tick-box," grudge expense, because they need to convince shareholders or insurance companies that they care about their assets and people. In reality, they don't believe anything will ever happen to them, and view security at best as a "black art," and worse as an unnecessary and unwelcome diversion from core business.

This is certainly part of the explanation. The lack of familiarity of the business management with what security really is: the supreme enabler. It is true that security is not considered as a noble portfolio.

Security Officers, Victims of Prejudices Inherited from Previous Lives

I think that prejudices against security run along the same lines as prejudices against the military or the police, at least in our Western societies. In my 10 years in the military as a subaltern officer I always noted a very ambivalent attitude toward what the army represents in terms of values. A mixture of envy, jealousy, fear, and distrust. The somewhat strange idea that soldiers are violent by nature, and should be kept hidden somewhere in boot camps or sent abroad to fight wars that interest none. Police are also met by ambivalent feelings. If police are perceived as people that put bad people behind bars, they are also people that you do not want to see around. What they represent is not something people feel comfortable with. For the *vulgum pecus*, police and soldiers represent some form of authority and external power. And, let us face it, human beings can tolerate authority but they never like it when this authority is directed at them during their time at work (which is a third of their life!). What, I believe, makes the matter worse is the fact that now that they have reinvented themselves in the private sector, these security people do not have the ability to proceed to an arrest, and they are, in fact, relatively powerless in front of other employees. Ex-soldiers never had that power, but the big difference is that they spent their life in a community ruled by regulations that all under uniform accept and practice. Military society is defined by strict rules that form the mind of the soldier. When turned into security officers and paid to implement security policies and procedures, that they cannot entirely enforce without a bit of diplomacy, they feel they are in an awkward situation and often turn confrontational. This usually does not go over very well with employees. Hence there is a tension that needs to be taken into account by the security executive in the security program.

Ignorance or Misconception about the Organization of Security

On top of this unconscious mistrust or wariness toward security people, there is, among the cadres in big organizations, a relative misconception about corporate security, its role and organization. One misconception is the difficulty of grasping that there could be different levels of competence in security—like in accountancy, for example. Discussing this issue with colleagues in the past, I realized that they could not understand what a career path in security could look like and did not understand why I had been recruited at a certain level, why my deputies were my deputies and not the contrary, and how excellent officers and foremen could be moved up the ladder. Obviously, they could not see which criteria could be used to promote someone in security, and I must admit that in those days, it was not always easy to explain. I remember, for example, that colleagues working as heads or security managers were always looking for courses that their officers could take, and I myself took a number of short courses that were on offer with serious organizations like S2 Institute, for example, and recommended them to the security officers. These courses were well done, brilliantly delivered, and accessible to all. The issue at that stage was to find a path for security officers to do something in addition to accumulating short on-line courses to improve their security knowledge and convince the management that these courses added some kind of value for the company's security posture. ASIS International and their trio of certifications—the CPP, the PSP, and the PCI—were often too tough for security officers and an intermediate level was missing then (which has since been filled, I think). For most employees of an organization, security is the place for those that cannot do anything, that have no skills, that cannot perform anything of value because they do not really have a job. In a company I worked for firefighters were paid three times more than security officers, while their schooling was comparable (and all security officers had received basic firefighting training!). As most security officers had served, they had a long arm of certifications regarding weapons handling and explosive training. They were all trained in observation techniques, were always neatly dressed and immaculate in their uniforms, could write good reports and yet, when as a director of security I tried to have their salary increased, I was told by the HR manager, "We can't do that. You know they're just security people, they have no real skills." The fact that identification of most safety issues is the result of night patrol by security officers and that these safety discoveries often represent thousands of dollars in savings, the image of security officers is such that they will be kept at the bottom of the salary list. I find this sad and unfair and it must change. The image of the security officer as physically strong and mentally wanting is an image deeply ingrained in the traditional employee's psyche. A security person, no matter his rank or level in the organization, is first and foremost a guard. With time, provided he behaves, he becomes a supervisor, puts a tie around his neck, and tries to appear business-like. But this is just a disguise that convinces no one. Deep down he remains a security officer and will remain so until he retires...again.

We all know how wrong this perception is. It may have been true at some stage, although I suspect that bad apples were always a minority in the profession and that security people have always tried to do their best with the means at their disposal. I recently watched a video on YouTube where an ATM somewhere in South Africa, by all means a very dangerous country to do cash-in-transit, was attacked by criminals armed with AK-47s while two security officers were changing the metallic boxes. Incredibly, one of the two guards in transit returned fire with a less than impressive pistol until, vanquished by the storm of steel discharged in his direction, he eventually abandoned the place to the criminals. I was stunned by the courage of this man, taken off guard while doing a routine task, thrown without notice into a deadly duel with superior power, who nevertheless refused to give in and flee like a frightened rabbit. I really admired his courage and I am sure that there are many men and women like this one in our profession.

There is nothing disgraceful about being a security officer, yet too many security officers feel despised and unloved. If officers—through commitment, hard work, and discipline—become security supervisors, it means that they have reached a level of skills needed to reach a modest but valuable management position. And they should not be ashamed of that. Yet, secretaries, other employees, even drivers, look down on them, because they seem to be idle, sitting behind counters and watching screens, when they do not bother everybody with forgotten badges, misplaced keys, unaccompanied visitors, and obsolete vehicle stickers.

This perception goes up to the highest echelons of society. Once, when I was invited to the residence of the French ambassador in Doha, the commercial attaché, once I gave him my business card, said to me, "Oh, you are in the security business? The *gendarme* who is here does not want to go back to France. Can you take him with you as a security guard?" I explained that unless he spoke Arabic or was fluent in English, he would not get a job in the region (and he was essentially a French speaker), and that in any case, I could not help because I was not involved in manguarding or cash-in-transit. I remember his amazed look while he tried to understand what I was telling him, explaining that my company was doing risk assessment, conceptual design, and security engineering. He frowned, grunted, and turned away, never to speak to me again, although I met him several times at the embassy after this exchange. I do not think he ever figured out what kind of security I was involved in, but obviously, it was not the security he had envisioned and he did not like it.

Another issue that generates this contempt—contempt might be a bit harsh, let us call it condescension—is due to the fact that security managers are often there as a second career. Ex-soldiers or ex-police, they are perceived of as the physical type, not the brainy kind. Often appearing rigid and overwhelming in their physical attitude, they rarely shine by their diplomatic skills, and this is seldom appreciated in organizations. It tends to confirm the preconception that security people are stubborn and rigid individuals that really do not add much value to business of the company. Yet, I am quite proud to say that the most sophisticated minds I have met in my life, I met in the military while I served as a reserve officer. I have never seen such a brilliant combination of reflection, commitment, and even a philosophical approach to the epistemology of risk, and life in general, among the officers I met in a short career spanning 10 years.

The last point is of course the main excuse to denigrate security people: their alleged lack of flexibility and their ignorance of the necessities of business. This, of course, is an nothing but an excuse. No one would think to criticize an accountant because she carefully checks the cash expenses of the senior managers. It is her job, after all. The difference with security people is that they are not perceived as being people who ensure protection—while they obviously are—but like stiff-minded people who enforce silly and unpleasant policies. Of course, some people are more prone to discipline than others, but broadly speaking, the security person is there to enforce regulations nobody believes in and make a fuss over irrelevant incidents.

What is our share of the responsibility for this state of affairs? Green believes that the industry itself is responsible for this image. He argues that:

> The security industry does precious little to combat this serious image issue. Steadfastly insisting on recruiting ex-combatants (no offence) or ex-police officers, results in a clear over-representation of reactive, retro-spective "fire-fighters" or investigators, rather than the predictive, pre-ventative mind sets required to deliver effective security. (Green, 2017)

What are the immediate solutions that come to mind if we want to change this sad state of affairs?

> Unless we start to see cadres of fresh-faced students coming out of uni-versities, clutching their degrees in criminology and risk management, and rushing into the nearest security firm, this situation will persist. And of course, the industry will need to offer packages that are attractive enough to tempt and then retain such bright sparks. (Green, 24 Aug 2017)

THE CORPORATE SOLUTION

Dr. Alison Wakefield, in a remarkable article titled "What Next for the Professionalization of Security,"[2] has perfectly summarized the reasons behind the poor perception of security people and where the solution lies. After acknowledging the traditional reasons behind the poor perception (reputation of secrecy, second career for many, ignorance of corporate security requirements, absence of qualifications), she proposes solutions that for middle-aged, second-career practitioners might come too late. Continuing professional development, a consensus on the body of knowledge, and a promotion of recognized certifications are indeed the road to follow and are already being pursued. But mentalities take time to change—they will in due course—and security will be accepted as a profession and the security manager as a full manager, thanks to the efforts of a handful of academics and professionals, but for now, I think security people practice wishful thinking in seeing themselves as the equivalent of other executives in the corporate environment. Do not get me wrong, though! The solutions envisaged to improve the perception of the security profession and the efforts by the academic community with dozens of degrees in security management and associations such as ASIS International in the US and the Security Institute in the UK with their professional certifications are highly commendable—and must be supported—I belong to both these organizations and have done so for many years and I am a CPP, a PSP, and a PCI—but the results of their efforts although already perceptible in the security profession will take some time before breaking the prejudices of the corporate world. To be honest, security executives, while supporting their professional associations, should be keen on looking after themselves without expecting too much from being a security management graduate and a certified practitioner.

This is why I would like to introduce in this chapter some concepts that will probably shock some readers who may just put the book away with scorn never to return to it. I beg them to read the few forthcoming pages with an open mind and simply refer to their own experience before discarding these principles as irrelevant to strategic security thinking.

I understand their reaction and might have reacted similarly a few years ago, before I really became interested in self-development.

THE INDIVIDUAL SOLUTION AND HOW IT ALL BEGAN

I discovered self-development quite by chance. Approximately 10 years ago, I applied for a course in rapid reading, which I thought would help me read faster on an academic level (I was embarked in a master's degree in international relations) and on a professional level (daily reading of newspapers to monitor the situation of the region I was working in). This course, organized by a Dubai-based company, was remarkable, well organized, and masterfully delivered, and I would recommend it to any security practitioner. We could measure daily our progress thanks to rapid reading exercises practiced with a reading machine that selected the line to be read at increasing speed. A questionnaire followed each test to make sure that the student had understood the content. The book that the instructor used for the speed-reading exercises was by Dobbins and Pettman, titled *What Self-Made Millionaires Really Think, Know and Do* (full reference at the end of the chapter). We did not read the whole book, obviously, but I found the selected portions used during the training quite intriguing and some of them even revealing. In spite of its catchy title, the purpose of the book was not to help its reader become a millionaire. Nobody really believes than by reading a book one will become a millionaire, but the book was teeming with ideas and concepts I had never heard of before, and quite logically, I bought it to know more. This book and its original approach to both personal life and business career strategy was a revelation. Of course, few of their assertions had a scientific flavor, but their statements had the irresistible attraction of logic and common sense.

149

Another source of guidance came from my willingness to improve my public speaking skills. Although I do not speak that often nowadays, I was quite involved at some stage with public speaking and training. I bought many books about ways to improve my voice, my attitude, and everything that would turn me into a great orator. Among these books where those written by Dale Carnegie, all of them written in the first half of the twentieth century but which have been regularly updated by Dale Carnegie Training and still sells very well today. Carnegie was the guru of public speaking of triumphant America and wrote many books on this issue. I realized by reading—and regularly rereading—his books that his approaches had been precursors of self-development techniques, although they were not labeled as such in those days.

Although neuro-linguistic programming (NLP), the buzz of the 1980s, has now been partially discredited in psychological circles, positive thinking remains very much in fashion: after all, thinking positively cannot be bad, can it? Business reviews fill regularly fill gaps in their articles with this seducing and comforting topic (particularly in July/August when nothing much happens in our world). The idea behind positive thinking is that it will not only improve your quality of life, but will also boost your attitude at work, and make you more prone to promotion. There is certainly something behind this idea and it is quite obvious that pleasant people have more chances of being selected for promotion than difficult, unsocial and really unpleasant employees. No need to write books about it, anybody could see that.

What was the idea behind positive thinking that made it a resounding success then? To put it simply, NLP posited that the positive use of words, and the rejection of negative sentences, would put you in a position to reach your goals faster and more effectively. As Lynn Williams once wrote, "Positive thinkers have a sense of purpose." She remarked that

> "Positive thinkers give much more of their time and attention to what is positive than to what is negative." However, they don't just look on the bright side; they take positive steps to ensure that there is ample bright side for them to look up to. Positive thinkers don't just think positively, they act positively too. They have a well-defined set of beliefs, attitudes and behaviors that are characteristic of them and contribute significantly to the way they act and the way they respond to life. (Williams 2009: ix)

The positive thinking derivative theory called neuro-linguistic programming took the business world by storm and people believed that anybody applying these simple word-related principles (always using positive

150

sentences, banning negative ideas, finding positive aspects to any set-backs) would make that person reach the apex of any organization. If that were possible, the pyramid would look quite funny, with a mass of positive thinking people at the top and a few losers left behind to do the work. Yet, there were some good things in NLP and I think that throw-ing the baby out with the bath water was a bit extreme. First, there was nothing intrinsically new in these principles. Andrew Carnegie, the guru of public speaking, based his training on similar principles. In his many books, still best-sellers, applications of positive thinking behav-ior abound. Modestly, he used to say that he did not invent anything but simply applied principles that Buddha, Jesus, and others had defined centuries ago. He was too modest. Carnegie intuitively understood that self-programming was key to influencing people, and by doing so, would improve one's position in the hierarchy of groups and organizations. It is probably through his books—that I bought to improve my public speaking performance—that I first discovered the basic principles of self-improvement.

USING THE MENTAL LAWS TO YOUR ADVANTAGE: HELPING DEFINE YOUR STRATEGY

During the last 20 years, hundreds of books has been written that encom-pass all aspects of self-development and the necessity of establishing personal, career, and development goals. Why such a chapter in this book since everything, or almost everything, has been written on such a topic? This chapter does not intend to replace this vast library of per-sonal improvement, but to open the eyes of practitioners who, in their vast majority, show little interest and/or do not believe in self-development. I cannot remember seeing any of my colleagues reading a self-help book during the lunch pause, or having one such book on their desk, or being interested in discussing personal career issues with me or any other professional.

This, I believe, is a major weakness. Not that I believe that reading such books will really make you rich and famous, but simply because this literature provides a framework for some reflection about yourself, and what you want to do with your career and your life. It forces you into thinking about the future and giving it some structure as well as deter-mining a direction. Last, it provides easy recipes to improve your self-confidence and, as consequence, your performance. I am no psychologist and will not cite psychological research to justify my position, but my point is to create an awareness and arouse curiosity toward a genre that can be of service to our profession. In their seminal book *What Self-Made Millionaires Really Think, Know and Do*, Dobbins and Pettman state that success is definitely linked to goal-setting. They quite convincingly suggest—and demonstrate—that setting goals for your career and for your personal life will make you a different person and help you achieve the goals you set, provided "you are prepared to set it as a goal and you are prepared to pay the price in advance" (Dobbins and Pettman 2006: 30). By paying the price in advance the authors mean learning the skills necessary to achieve these goals.

Establishing goals definitely requires a strategic attitude and as such, it has its rightful place in this book on strategy. It is even, I think, the exact definition of it. What do I want, where do I want to go, and how am I going to get there from where I am now? The most important element of the Dobbins and Pettman book is, I think, the idea of responsibility. This idea, as simple as it is, is the foundation to any project. As Carnegie highlighted: "You should certainly accept responsibility for yourself, and you should even be able to accept it for other people when they are not in a position to do so" (Carnegie 2011: 11). Nothing new for those who have served; the chief is responsible for everything, even things he knows nothing about. This statement once shocked all subalterns until it became in turn their motto. But for a younger generation coming out of university, it may not seem obvious. Yet, it must be an absolute rule for you, in your career as well as in life. Why? Because to accept responsibility is to take control.

The second principle is that every goal is reachable if you believe in it, are ready to make it a goal, and are ready to pay the price in advance. It follows a simple fact that you are where you are because of what you did, and that if you change nothing in your life, you will remain exactly where you are. This seems pretty obvious, but I think it is worth highlighting. Thus, "if you want to be somewhere else in 3 years in the future, then you must go and work on your knowledge/skills and your attitude." (Dobbins and Pettman 2006: 37). Skills and attitude will make the difference. But do not be led into thinking that modifying one's attitude is something easy. It is easier to acquire skills and knowledge than to change one's attitude. Working on the skills is something easy to decide: "I need to be a CPP, or a PSP, or get a degree in security management, or an MBA, if I want to get the job I think I deserve." Once you've signed up for a program, you just have to show determination and discipline and with patience and tenacity you will get there. It demands commitment, certainly, but many of us—particularly middle-aged practitioners—are capable of impressive commitment and have often proved it in our lives. Changing your attitude from a blasé attitude to a dynamic and positive one is a work of each instant. With a contrite heart, I must admit that I still battle with that. I must constantly remind myself that I need to smile more and be friendlier with people, fellow employees and customers alike. It does not come to me naturally. Does it bring results? This is a very good question. People take for granted that being a nice person will help you succeed. It is a possibility, but there is no guarantee in life…The same goes for being sincere, really caring about people. I do not know whether it is effective and whether it can help you in your career. What I do know is that dealing with positive, caring, and honest people is more pleasant than dealing with obnoxious and unpleasant people. So, if by applying these principles you make yourself a nicer person to others, why not do it? It cannot harm you, can it? Being positive can only have positive consequences, so go for it!

THE SUCCESS FORMULA AND THE LAWS THAT WILL HELP YOU

I borrow again from Dobbins and Pettman, because this equation needs to be really ingrained in your brains from now on. Success does not depend on your intelligence, connections, diplomas, or other things you hear everywhere. Or rather it does not depend *only* on these factors. Success depends on only two factors:

knowledge/skills × attitude = results/performance

Another illuminating remark by Dobbins and Pettman was, "if you stay as you are, you stay where you are. The more you do of what you do, the more you get of what you have got" (Dobbins and Pettman 2006: 9).

Dobbins and Pettman list a number of mental laws I will briefly discuss now. Here is a quick summary of each law.

The Law of Belief

This law says that you are what you believe you are. In other words, if you think you are good at selling, you are good at selling. If you believe you are a security genius, you are—somehow—a security genius.

153

You may not have mastered the skills necessary to become the security expert you want to be, but if you believe you are a security expert, you will make the efforts necessary to become that expert. However, if you repeatedly say, "I am unlucky, I do not do well at exams," these limiting beliefs will also become your reality. This is where *positive thinking cum NLP* has a role to play.

Long before the golden age of cognitive psychology, a French pharmacist called Emile Coué (1857–1926) introduced a popular method of psychotherapy and self-improvement based on optimistic autosuggestion. Coué was the precursor of Napoleon Hill and other Americans influenced by his book *Self-Mastery through Conscious Autosuggestion*, published in England (1920) and in the U.S. (1922). An important point highlighted by Dobbins and Pettman is that "you can believe anything that you want to believe" (Dobbins and Pettman 2006: 44). Your beliefs become your reality. Thus, if you want to change your perception of yourself, you need to change your beliefs about yourself. Transform your image of your current self into that of a successful executive and you will believe in skills that you may not possess as yet but that you will acquire, because you want to. Remember, you always need to pay the price in advance. The good thing about changing your beliefs in such a way is that you will create positive expectations for yourself that will immediately and naturally translate into positive attitudes. Try to focus on positive beliefs and positive expectations, and positive emotions will follow. As Henry Ford once said, "whether you think you will succeed or not, you are right."

The Law of Cause and Effect

The law of cause and effect stipulates that if you want something to happen, you must constantly think about it and make it a goal (and a belief). It is often said that thinking about something is the first step in its realization, and if you decide to change your goals and look in a new direction, you will draw it toward your reality. Think therefore about your strategic goals, tangible of course—the house you want, the car you desire—but also intangible such as the success or the admiration you crave from other people such as colleagues or friends. The idea is therefore to establish your strategic goals for your career, personal development, and private life. And from then on think about them. Write them down, and reread them regularly. These goals are not written in stone, though. I recently found goals I had written in 2010 and many of them are not that important to me today. Circumstances have changed and the total unpredictability of life has taken me to places I could not even imagine then. This is not important. These goals are guidelines for success, and guidelines for success keep you on the path to achievement. Your goals can change, and conditions and circumstances can change too and force you and your goals into unexpected directions, but your determination must not waver, and your commitment toward the acquisition of skills and knowledge should remain unchanged, until a goal has been reached, or changed.

The Law of Attraction

"The law of attraction postulate that there is an almost magnetic force which draws into our lives the information, circumstances and people in harmony with our dominant thoughts" (Dobbins and Pettman 2006:47). Indeed, by focusing on your personal goals, you will automatically attract to your sphere a new breed of people that can bring you knowledge, a greater vision of your job, and the potential for opportunities and change. The first time I experienced this was when I prepared for the CPP exam and studied at CNA-Q University in Qatar once a week with other security managers that became lifelong friends (thanks to LinkedIn, I admit), and met some extraordinary Canadian instructors, like the fantastic Dennis Shepp, now in semi-retirement in his native Canada! This preparation opened gates for me, created a new network of security professionals that is still very active in my region, pushed me into becoming an ASIS International member, and encouraged me to become a committee member as well as an instructor for CPP applicants at a later stage. It is not exactly the recipe to becoming a millionaire but it definitely helped me establish myself in the world of industrial security for the rest of my career. Talking about positive attitude...Dennis Shepp, CPP, PCI, was the most enthusiastic trainer and public speaker I have ever met and an influential mentor for a whole generation of security executives. He was, and still is, a shining example of how positive thinking makes one a better person.

The Law of Correspondence

The law of correspondence stipulates that the world we see around us is a reflection of our thoughts. Although it seems a bit extreme, isn't it quite true that reality is a reflection of our beliefs? Indeed, the way we perceive things is really influenced by our thoughts. Is our government corrupt? Is communism a murderous and unjust system? Was Che Guevara a

155

romantic and generous figure, or a terrorist? What we believe about things is how we approach reality. In other words, to reach your goals you must change your beliefs and adopt new thoughts, information, circumstances, people, and books that will help you become the person you want to become. Dobbins and Pettman suggest that to achieve this change you must use visualization, emotionalization, and affirmation to assist you in succeeding in the accomplishment of your targets. In practical terms: (1) Visualize = see the perfect outcome, what you want to be; (2) Emotionalize = close your eyes and imagine the feeling that you will have once you have reached your goal—feel yourself in the glass office on the 24th floor, or reading on a beach in an exclusive resort in the Indian Ocean, or playing golf at St. Andrews in Scotland; and (3) Affirm = I want to be regional security manager for the whole of Asia and make $200,000 a year. I know this one seems a bit far-fetched, but there is probably no harm in trying it and it will put you in the right direction.

The Law of Expression

The law of expression postulates that "whatever is impressed into your mind is expressed into your reality. Every idea or thought either drives you towards the achievement of your goals, or takes you away from the achievement of your goals, but nothing is neutral" (Dobbins and Pettman 2006: 51). In other words, you must from now on focus a great deal of your time on thinking about your goals, your personal development, and family objectives. What this means, in practical terms, is that if you want to reach your objectives, you must start cutting out TV programs, idle time spent in bars, and reading newspapers that really provide very little information—I personally read my tablet for 15 minutes in the morning while having breakfast, and I feel I know enough about "what's happening out there." You should also privilege public transport over cars, unless, of course, you listen to educational tapes.

One of my goals having been for some time to write this book, I have a laptop constantly with me and open it to work as soon as I am in an airport, a hotel, or anywhere I can use some spare time constructively.

Another important point here is that we are affected by those who surround us and tend to adopt their values, their beliefs, and alas, their attitudes. Think therefore about spending time with people who have goals and objectives, people with a purpose. By creating a mastermind alliance, you will have a feeling of doing the right thing and get closer to your life goals. Goal setting has already put you in the minority. With the law of expression, you put yourself higher on the professional and social ladder. Develop a program for self-development. Think about your job and how it is evolving. Try to think about what security will look like in 10 years. These qualifications that you acquired, and that seemed, at the time, the certifications to get, will they still mean something? Should you not go technical? Embrace cyber security? Is it what you want? Then you need to start working for technical certifications right now, even if you do not feel inclined toward technical studies. If you feel that this is the way to go, you must go! Adding to your knowledge while improving your overall attitude will make you stand out from the crowd. And choose good models and mentors. If you prepare for a CISA or CISM certification, for example, you will meet people that are often different from the physical security practitioners you are accustomed to meeting. This will open doors and windows of opportunity and help you create a new, parallel network of professional people. It takes 5 years to master a discipline, usually, and this is why if you feel you need to change tack, you must write down a program and stick to it. Making a decision and acting should guide your attitude.

The Law of Expectations

The law of expectations, as you now can guess, stipulates that you can achieve what you confidently expect to achieve. This means that you create your own limits to what you think you can achieve. This is not bad in itself, but it can be improved by increasing your attitude, boosting your self-image, and therefore elevating what you can confidently expect to achieve. By working on your attitude, you will increase your self-confidence and therefore your own level of expectations. The secret is in the attitude. Think positively and act confidently, and you will have higher expectations for your self.

The Law of Control

There is a direct link between control and responsibility. You remember we said that the first thing you have to do if you want to achieve your business, development, and personal goals is to accept responsibility. All leaders are ultimately responsible, and you must try to think and act the way they do. Stop making excuses, thinking that your current situation is the result of an external locus of control (economy, your boss, your spouse, your education) and accept full responsibility for where you are and by doing so get control of your life. Since you have the power to feed your mind with new knowledge and skills, and to work on a new, more positive attitude, you will get control of your life in the domains that are important for you. As Dobbins and Pettman aptly remark, "you are the only person who can learn creativity, goal-setting, strategy, marketing, sales skills, negotiation, leadership, finance and time management" (Dobbins and Pettman 2006: 55). Success, and more to the point, happiness, are associated with the fulfilling sensation that you are now, entirely and consciously, the master of your destiny.

The Law of Accumulation

The law of accumulation says that creativity creates more creativity, money begets more money, knowledge produces more knowledge, and so on (and failure begets more failure, alas). This is something that popular wisdom imparted long ago and it probably results from simple observation. This, of course, will apply to you, but as I have said earlier, there is a price to pay. You cannot spend your evening in front of the TV, and your weekends at the rugby club and expect things to change. This is what brought you where you are and, if you do not change it, this is where you are going to stay. If you make the decision to work on your personal development, health, family relationship, and so on then things will improve. Make the decision to take the course in business continuity that is being offered nearby, volunteer to take a CPP training, or join your chapter and propose to help teach the CPP course for new security professionals. Think that by doing and by volunteering, you will make yourself tougher and that, very quickly, you will stop going to the club when you return from work because you will have better things to learn or to teach. While you work on this behavioral change, you will also notice that you will envy the success of others less and less, because you feel that what you do is valuable and makes you a better person. Be realistic in your expectations, be focused, but act. Action and attitude are the secrets. Start gathering now all the things that you think will help you achieve your goals in the future.

The Law of Concentration

This is an interesting one, because, I must admit, I first found it hard to believe. It stipulates that the more you concentrate on your goals, the quicker your goals will be achieved. Obviously, you need to believe in it and it is not that obvious. This is why most self-help authors suggest writing your strategic goals (5 years) on your computer and then read them every day. Reading these goals every day, visualizing the outlook, emotionalizing, and affirming should bring results. It has not totally worked for me yet, but I must admit that I lack discipline, and if I am good at setting goals, I am less good at coping with the psychological stuff that goes with the process. It is certainly credible that focus and concentration will activate the subconscious in some way and that this unconscious concentration has more ability to bring the right information and the right behavior to reach your goals, than watching a TV program or discussing nonsense at the pub.

The Law of Reversibility

The law of reversibility seems to me more a technique than a law. It suggests visualizing the perfect outcome, whatever you want it to be, and trying to reverse engineer and imagine the path you that brought you to this outcome, the situations you were in, the decisions you took, and so on. In simple words, what were the steps that you must have taken to reach the ideal point you reached? It is interesting and requires some focus. It is difficult to put in place, because you have different kinds of goals, and for each goal there might be a myriad of probabilities and possible choices that make the exercise difficult. I have personally never tried it and find it a bit overwhelming. Although I find it a difficult technique to implement, I have kept it in the list because I believe it has value.

The Law of Substitution

The law of substitution suggests that when assailed by negative thoughts, you should replace them with positive ones. This technique, suggested by Dobbins and Pettman, consists of concentrating on your personal and career goals. This focus should fill you with positive emotions of excitement and enthusiasm. With practice, you can substitute all the negative emotions one goes through in one's daily life and adopt a positive mental attitude. Dobbins and Pettman are excellent at finding examples and suggestions and I do not want to substitute poor examples for good ones.

The Law of Habit

This law is again another way to approach positive thinking. It simply stipulates that acquiring knowledge/skills combined with a positive attitude should become a habit.

The Law of Emotion

We already touched on the issue of emotion a bit earlier in this chapter. Emotion is a great enabler. And this law of emotion is a technique that I have been practicing for some time. My PhD was a long and painful process and it took me more than 6 years to complete after my master's degree. When I felt depressed, I watched the graduation ceremonies on my university's website and read the comments. There was, at some stage, on the day of the graduation, the Pimm's of the dean, and as I drink Pimm's too rarely, I regularly closed my eyes and could smell the aperitif. I could imagine myself in gown and Tudor bonnet, drinking my Pimm's with the intellectual elite of my university if not with the vice-chancellor himself. This thought did not make me finish my PhD earlier, but it did help me stay focused and on course. I know it is vain, but it helped. As you can guess, on the day of my graduation, I realized that the Pimm's of the dean as a tradition had ceased to exist. Not such a big disappointment after all, since it was graduation day and I enjoyed every minute of it. As an emotional enabler, the dean's aperitif had perfectly fulfilled its role!

This raises an important point. If emotion is an important drive, the realization of the reward may not be necessary. I was speaking with my boss this morning, discussing a car he promised himself he would buy if he managed to make an important sale. He told me that getting the car of his dreams as a reward for success had really been important all along. Yet, once he had reached his goal, the idea of getting this car did not seem that important after all, and he eventually decided that he did not need it. This example confirms that emotionalization can be an extraordinary motivator.

The Law of Superconscious Activity

This law stipulates that "any thought, wish, desire or goal which you can hold consistently in your mind must be brought into your reality by your superconscious" (Dobbins and Pettman 2006: 62). For Dobbins and

Pettman, the superconscious is the source of innovation, creativity, excitement, and blinding flashes of the obvious. The superconscious responds to clarity, strong emotion and desire, authority, and positive affirmations. It is activated by solitude and concentration. I am a strong believer in the superconscious and noticed long ago that when faced with a problem, a long walk or a longer run usually provided a solution I could not see under normal circumstances. The superconscious works for you. Ask him for solutions when you are facing a wall. Some authors suggest that on top of clarity you give orders to your superconscious like "I want an answer to this problem by the end of the week." I have not gone that far, but would not be surprised if it does work. Michalko suggests that taking a break and forgetting about a problem allows the information to come back and grow clearer. Cognitive scientists have observed that after a period of incubating their ideas, people are 33% more likely to infer connections among distantly related ideas. Yet, this enhancement of creative thinking occurs completely beneath the radar—people are more creative after they forget about a problem for a period of time, but they do not know it. It is as if the period of incubation resets your mind. You are talking a walk or taking a shower and you realize "Wait a minute, there is another way to do it!" (Michalko 2011: 132). This is superconscious work at its best and I think we have all experienced this phenomenon. Michalko cites Bertrand Russel:

> I have found, for example, that if I have to write upon some rather difficult topic, the best plan is think about it with very great intensity—the greatest intensity of which I am capable—for a few hours, or days, and at the end of that time give orders, so to speak, that the work is to proceed underground. After some months, I return consciously to the topic and find that the work has been done. Before I had discovered this technique, I used to spend the intervening months worrying because I was making no progress; I arrived at the solution no sooner for this worry, and the intervening months were wasted. (cited in Michalko 2006: 134)

You must believe in the power of your subconscious. The more you really want to solve the problem and are ready to fully concentrate on it with "the greatest intensity you are capable of" the more likely it is that your subconscious will provide solutions.

The Law of Compensation

In life, we are rewarded for the quality and quantity of service we provide to others. Working more hours at doing what you do may help you slightly improve your condition. If you want to *dramatically* improve your situation, the solution lies in the quality of what you do and not its quantity. How is this achievable? Again, it is achievable by increasing your knowledge/skills and by adopting a better mental attitude. How to change your situation? By doing more before 9 and after 5. We need to commit to helping others, become mentors, and/or be part of a cultural or sports club. In simple words, we need to give to others if we want to be rewarded in return.

The Law of Reciprocity

This law says that as human beings, we tend to want to help those who help us. It is a bit strange to think that one way to achieve your objectives is to take some of your precious time to help others achieve theirs, and yet there is an undeniable correlation between the help we provide and the support we receive. It is a bit weird at the beginning but you eventually get used to giving to others, preparing courses to help younger colleagues achieve certifications, providing support at work, putting your experience at the service of others, becoming a mentor. You will be perceived as a generous and committed person, and if there is a possibility of return, you will benefit from it. Give and you will be given.

The Law of Inertia

The law of inertia, inherited from the world of physics, says that a body that is not stimulated by an external force will stay where it is. Inertia is comfortable, but inertia is incompatible with setting goals and reaching them. Inertia can be observed in many offices and facilities where people keep the same job for decades. Inertia is what you want to avoid at all cost, because inertia generates negative thoughts, and negative thoughts are the perfect excuse for career failures. Inertia is therefore your enemy. You need to set yourself in motion by setting you goals and taking steps toward their achievement.

PATIENCE, THE MOTHER OF ALL VIRTUES

All these mental laws and techniques are therefore tools to be put at the service of your goal-setting and -achievement. Of course, all is not as simple as it sounds here, and things have to be understood in the context of the long span. Not all this will happen overnight and there is advice that needs to be considered before embarking on the process of goal achievement. The most difficult part of goal-setting is goal-setting itself. It can be something difficult to articulate, particularly for younger people. For the older audience, the most difficult thing to acquire will be to understand that goal-achieving cannot be reached overnight and takes an irritating amount of time. Patience, the mother of all virtues, must be learned, understood, and integrated in one attitude.

Patience can be defined as the ability to wait without experiencing anger, anxiety, or frustration. Now that you have, at last, written your goals and integrated the ideas behind the mental laws that will help you reach these goals, you may think that the process of achievement goes without saying and will happen overnight, or quite. Alas, life has its own pace, and you have to accept that. Your life, even with well-defined objectives, will not be a constant walk to success. You must continue accepting the vicissitudes that are part of a normal life. You also need to take into account that the famous "price to pay in advance" takes time. It takes months and commitment to prepare for certifications, and it takes years to get a degree, particularly when you do it part time, and still work full time. And do not forget that results will start being perceptible only when these objectives have been reached after a reasonable latency—the time that people around you integrate your recent achievement and its significance. One has therefore to be patient if you need a degree to do a particular job and it will take you 5 years to obtain it. In other words, even if you have set career, development, and private goals, there is no need to rush yourself into getting immediate results—that you will not get anyway—and you must learn to be patient, with others of course, but mainly with yourself. Patience will avoid nurturing growing frustrations such as I now have a degree and do not receive more interesting job offers. This is not how life works and if mental laws will help you focus and reach your objectives, they will not work miracles.

There is some advice that I can give you and that you will also find in many self-development books on this topic. First accept the idea that there are things that you cannot control or influence. Try to spend the most time on things you can control, because this is what will make a difference in your life. Do not be too harsh on yourself. Once our goals are set and we have done everything that we planned to do, we want to rush into things, and we become impatient. In your life, you will keep making mistakes, there will be incidents, and setbacks will hamper your progress. Everybody makes mistakes. Everybody has to face unforeseen issues, and there is no straight line to success. What will make you different from most people is that you will learn from these problems and remain focused.

Something important that needs to be mentioned is that when you plan your goals, you follow an achievement plan. Yet, this plan is not carved in stone. You may need to reorientate your life for many unforeseen reasons. The things that you cannot control may prevent you from reaching goals that no longer make sense. You must not be stubborn. Remember the purpose is to go somewhere, learn, digest, change tack eventually, and move forward. Always have a plan B at the ready, in case circumstances make your original plan undoable, or because you decide on another course of action. If you persist in something that becomes unattainable, you will create anger, anxiety, and frustration, all negative thoughts that you have decided to ban long ago. Confront your feelings about not achieving immediate success. Focus on small steps that encourage you toward your objectives, and do not hesitate to alter these objectives if circumstances beyond your control make their achievement too difficult. To avoid anxiety and anger, you must feel that the goals, even if they at first appear far away, are there to be taken.

SERENDIPITY

Most self-development writers, and Dobbins and Pettman are no exception, suggest that you plan your goals, and from there, create a to-do list that you follow scrupulously until you reach success. This is fine, but a bit extreme. Because as Adair aptly remarks, "being over organised, planning your life down to the last minute like a control freak, is inimical to creativity. For chaos often breeds creativity" (Adair 2009: 28). We will discuss creativity and its difficult relationship with security.

I think that one should plan goals, and keep these goals as a guideline. Serendipity is making unexpected and delightful discoveries by accident. It is about finding valuable and agreeable ideas or things, or people, when you are not consciously looking for them. I think this process is inherent to human nature, and once your goals are established you must be flexible and open-minded, and practice a comfortable serendipity.

Lord Grocott, the then chancellor of the University of Leicester, said during a moving speech at my graduation ceremony, "if there is one thing I get from life, it is its absolute unpredictability!" Serendipity gives you this open-mindedness that will help the superconscious find a way toward the *spirit of your goals*. It may not be exactly what you wanted but it may be worth it. As Christopher Milne said:

> You can decide exactly what you want to do, and make a list on a piece of paper and then do it all precisely. [...] Or you can have a rough idea of what you want, hope to set off in the right direction and probably end up with something quite different. Then you realise it is not such a bad thing after all. (Adair 2009: 27)

ASSERTIVENESS: TO BE OR NOT TO BE

That is a very interesting question, indeed. Books on assertiveness base their work on the premise that being assertive is a positive thing. As Lindenfield wrote:

> Assertiveness is used to describe a certain [type] of behaviour. It is behaviour which helps us to communicate clearly and confidently our needs, wants and feelings to other people without abusing in any way their human rights. (Lindenfield 2014: 3)

This sounds fine and to the point. Yet, it us not entirely convincing. Having worked on several continents and in diverse human and cultural environments, I have to say that such a vision of assertiveness is particularly Eurocentric. Even in our Western context, the limits of what is acceptable in terms of assertiveness may vary tremendously. It is an entirely personal notion and an someone seen as assertive by many may be perceived as an unbearable bully from another perspective. Let us begin by defining the word, a not so straightforward exercise. Dictionary.com defines an assertive person as someone who is *confidently aggressive or self-assured*. The *Cambridge English Dictionary* defines assertive behavior as someone *behaving confidently and able to say in a direct way what they want or believe*. Last, for *Merriam Webster*, an assertive person is someone disposed to or characterized by *bold or confident statements and behaviour*. Again, a balanced attitude toward fellow employees and supervisors might be the solution. Few books on assertiveness emphasize this. Usually, once this premise has been established, the authors tell you that, in order to become that successful person that

165

nobody can resist, you must apply a number of techniques to make yourself more influential and more powerful through assertiveness. These ideas are not really new, and I feel no shame in exposing them, because they are simply principles that were already explored almost a century ago by Dale Carnegie.[3] For Carnegie, the way to improve your situation, developing self-confidence and influencing people, was through public speaking. He wrote many books on this topic, and all of them have something to contribute to the acquisition of self-confidence. Public speaking is indeed one way to improve your assertiveness and I must say that it really helped me a lot in my job. At some stage I spoke on anything I was asked to, provided it had something to do with corporate or industrial security. I think public speaking could be one way for you to develop your assertiveness—although *self-confidence* might be a more exact word But it is not the only way. Carnegie reflects on self-confidence in almost all of his books and the most recent one, a collective work produced by a group of authors at Carnegie Training, still emphasises the point. To sum up, it may be good to be assertive, but the limits of assertiveness are not clear-cut. Furthermore, assertiveness is a very culturally tainted notion. Be careful if you work in a multicultural environment to differentiate what could constitute assertiveness and what will be perceived as aggressive behavior. The difference may be infinitesimal, and have serious consequences for the image people will have of you.

COURAGE, THE ULTIMATE VIRTUE, AND THE FEAR OF FAILURE

Setting goals for a better and more exciting life is all good. And we all agree that goals should be realistically attainable. From there, it is really a free for all. Writing "In 3 years I want to be the VP of security in my organization," although it is a most valuable objective, does not reflect the same commitment as "In 3 years, I want to run my own consultancy in Xville, and have no debts." The first one does not apparently require a specific amount of moral courage. The second does, to a considerable extent. The first one, if not attained, may be postponed and reset as an objective on the 5-year horizon. The second one implies several things: the courage to leave an unsatisfying but paying job (for example) but also the real possibility of failure and its terrible consequences on family life. One is a goal that is framed in a normal career evolution; the second one is one of extreme risk and serious potential consequences. These goals therefore cannot be compared. Yet both can be considered as realistic. The main difference, in my opinion, is that the first one, if not reached, can be ignored. Your colleagues may not even be aware of it. The second one is a goal you cannot keep to yourself. It is an act of such courage that it cannot go unnoticed. To start a new business, you will have to resign and sign up for uncertainty. My purpose is not to judge you or to encourage you one way or the other. It is to tell you to consider what your chances are of reaching your goal. Are you good at selling, have you got the right network, will your former boss help you in this venture by subcontracting some work to you?

I would again follow advice from Dobbins and Pettman: do not make anything brutal. Start working on the side, prepare your exit, acquire the necessary skills and expand your network, and go from one situation to the other with a minimum of risk. Take your time and never, never burn your boats!

In our world of security, one needs to keep a friendly relationship with both colleagues and customers. This must be your number one rule. Make everything work to your advantage and whatever your choice of goal, let the laws and principles of success work for you.

And never, never, never give up! Reorientate, reschedule, revisit, and transform your goals if they have been too optimistic or if you have changed your mind about what you really want, but move forward with patience and determination.

SUMMARY

Security is suffering from a poor image in the C-suite and you, as a security executive, have to live with this situation. On top of consolidating your skills and abilities with degrees and certifications, it would be wise to apply what Dobbins and Pettman call *the laws of success*, a number of self-development/confidence-building techniques that will help make you more conspicuous and consequently more prone to internal promotion.

MAIN POINTS

- Because of the poor image of security, your technical capabilities as a security practitioner may not be sufficient to guarantee a career progression comparable to those enjoyed by other heads of department in the organization.
- Immerse yourself in the mental laws listed in this chapter, make them yours, and use them as career and life guidelines.
- Believe in these laws, and apply them as a second nature. Remember: knowledge/skills × attitude = results/performance
- Prepare for success by being ready to pay the price in advance, in other words, get the qualifications that will be necessary to your promotion up the ladder. It will be too late to prepare for a master's degree when a job that requires a master's degree in security becomes available. Get a CPP as soon as possible, as it has become a requirement for any security management position. Anticipate and work for it!
- Remember that even if you have ticked all the boxes, no change will happen overnight. Patience, the mother of all virtues, is needed to let the new your become known to others.
- Be open to serendipity. Do not become entangled in your set goals. Be flexible and receptive to opportunities. Remember that life—in spite of your best efforts—remains utterly unpredictable.
- Be yourself, and set goals you feel comfortable with and that are achievable. Do not over- or underestimate your courage.
- Be assertive, but more importantly be yourself. Nobody can play a role for very long. Be comfortable with yourself, with your goals, and share your enthusiasm with those around you.

END NOTES

1. Stephen Green is a Chartered Security Professional (CSyP), the highest level of recognition a security practitioner can reach in the UK.
2. In the Handbook of Security, edited by Prof. Martin Gill, see references at the end of the chapter.
3. Dale Carnegie started his courses in public speaking in 1912 and continued until his death in 1955.

REFERENCES

Adair, J. (2009) *The Art of Creative Thinking: How to be Innovative and Develop Great Ideas.* Kogan Page: London, UK.

Dale Carnegie & Associates (2011) *Make Yourself Unforgettable: How to Become the Person Everyone Remembers and No One Can Resist.* Simon & Schuster: New York.

Dobbins, R. & Pettman, B. O. 3rd ed. (2006) *What Self-Made Millionaires Really Think, Know and Do: A Straight-Talking Guide to Business Success and Personal Riches.* Capstone: Chichester, UK.

Lindenfield, G. 3rd ed. (2014) *Assert Yourself: Simple Steps to Build your Confidence.* Harper Thornsons: London, UK.

Michalko, M. (2011) *Creative Thinkering, Putting your imagination to work.* New World Library: Novato, CA.

Wakefield, A. (2014) Where next for the professionalization of security in M. Gill, ed., *The Handbook of Security*, 2nd ed. Palgrave Macmillan: New York, pp. 919–935.

Williams, L. (2009) *Perfect Positive Thinking: All You Need to Know.* RH Books: London, UK.

7

Creative Thinking and Security

CAN A SECURITY EXECUTIVE BE CREATIVE?

If everything ends up with songs, most things start with ideas! Let us face it, security practitioners are seldom perceived as creative people, and yet, there is no reason why thinking creatively should not be part of the security practitioner's approach. Dobbins and Pettman define creativity as "the ability to improve" (Dobbins and Pettman 2006: 3). Although it suits my purpose in this chapter, it is quite distant from the idea that one traditionally associates with creativity, which is often defined as the capacity to create something unique (artists and inventors immediately come to mind as examples of creative people, while pilots, surgeons, and lawyers do not). However, creativity may simply be the capacity to improve things, in some way, over which we have some control.

Creativity as a way of improving things should therefore be part of our professional skills, and we are going to suggest a few methods, some I have tested, others I have not, that will help you become more creative and probably a little bit more effective.

THE DETERMINANTS OF CREATIVITY

Using some of the mental laws to your advantage can stimulate your creativity. To start with, you must convince yourself that you are a creative person. Remember? Visualize, emotionalize, and affirm. Start repeating aloud: "I am a creative person." This is where it all begins. Then, provide your employees with an environment that is encouraging, positive, and exciting. Excitement, even at work, is a very positive emotion (Dobbins and Pettman 2006: 5) and emotions are vectors of self-esteem, a sentiment strongly associated with creativity. So, in encouraging your personnel and making them feel valuable, you help create an environment propitious to creativity, yours but also your team's. This is an important point, since, in the running of your security department, your cadres will be involved in brainstorming sessions that will help you upgrade the current security posture. Your duty, as a manager, is to make sure that your security workforce feels useful, valued, and respected. Creating such an environment is one of your main duties as a manager.

Another determinant of a creative approach to security will be to establish clear goals with specific deadlines. Having an objective and a deadline stimulates thought and breeds creativity.

Another way to stimulate a creative spirit in your team is to be conscious of the limiting factors your department and you yourself are going to face. Often, these limitations live only in the minds of others and your supervisor. VPs and CSOs are not immune to misconceptions of what security should be. The limiting image of security as a function comes immediately to mind. The guard-at-the-gate image stands strong in management spirits. Another hurdle could be a lack of financial independence (I worked for 4 years as a director of security without a proper budget for my activities—talk about frustration!); it can be a lack of leadership from your immediate authority; it can also be an inadequate, or poorly recruited or trained, workforce, and/or the total absence of any strategy for the security department (a very common ailment!). You must think about these factors while you initiate a SWOT exercise with your team.

The most important factor, as emphasised by Michalko, is that "you become what you pretend to be and that intention breeds creativity." Said simply, you must affirm without any doubt that you are a creative person, and you will become one. You must then have the intention of using this creativity for specific purposes to understand the magnitude of its real potential.

PRINCIPLES OF CREATIVE THINKING:
CLARITY, CLARITY, AND CLARITY

Thinking creatively does not mean that you will invent new ways of doing security and applying security principles. Thinking creatively is simply a way of thinking positively, of taking responsibility and of taking your personnel with you in new directions. The secret of creative thinking is open-mindedness, a flexibility in your approach, a clearly optimistic attitude toward your work, and a solution-orientated rather than a problem-focussed type of thinking. The principle to follow is to adopt a positive, flexible, and intelligent approach to security issues. This means accepting ideas different from yours and being able to brainstorm with your team and use techniques to get the best of what the team is able to produce in terms of solutions to security challenges. One of the principles of creative thinking that stems from the mental laws we discussed in the previous chapter is that to become a master of creative thinking you must believe, and affirm, "I am a creative person." If you do not believe that you are—or that you can become such a person—you are wasting your time and will carry on working as you always have.

Thinking with clarity about an issue is one of the main points in finding a solution to a problem and the first to start with. It is often said that posing a problem with clarity is solving half of it. When faced with a specific problem (that you must call a challenge, by the way, and not a problem!), try and see the big picture. See which causes created the challenge and, irrespective of the current deadlock, what would be the perfect outcome. In other words, try to clearly identify the path to that outcome and then try to identify the obstacles that prevent you, and your department, from reaching it. Establish goals and point with clarity to the different actions (that would become milestones of a sort) that could be taken to reach that goal. Think out loud, or in group. Be realistic, identify the solutions to the individual hurdles, find ways to get rid of them, always follow the least complicated way, and act. Often the suppression of one issue along the way will have a domino effect that might solve most of the issue. But work with a method, step by step, and do not try to cut corners on principle. It is a bad habit!

Getting rid of hurdles one after another in the direction of travel is one approach. Another one is to keep the perfect outcome in sight and reverse engineer the process from where you want to be to where you are right now. Starting from the outcome, endeavor to visualize what steps took

173

you to the result. It is a difficult exercise, but a good one, since it forces you to think and think hard. My grandmother always told me, "The best is the enemy of good." Surprisingly, she was wrong. Good is the enemy of best, because when you have found an acceptable solution, you stop thinking about a better one. Accepting a good, acceptable solution is something you must fight constantly. Go for the best solution, no matter what efforts it requires. Make lists, concentrate on the steps that need to be achieved, and stay focused. The concentration will determine your success.

Last, do not get attached to an idea solely because it is yours. You may be biased on one topic or your experience may push you toward solutions that may not be the ones required in the current situation, or you may not have any valuable experience regarding a specific issue, but you think that since you are the boss, you have to come up with something. This is not the way to go. Keep an open mind. Consult and listen to others. Not only your people, as others may have solutions for your issues because they experienced similar problems in other regions of the world. I remember that a few years ago, my company had been victim of repeated thefts of solar panels in block-valve stations located in a desert environment, along a gas pipeline crossing several countries. We were thinking about ways to reinforce the nuts and bolts or to fence the panels, when, after a weekly management meeting, the VP of operations told me that they had faced the same problem in Indonesia and that they had to think hard before finding the solution that prevented the recurrence of such thefts. This was nothing complicated or spectacular and it was certainly not costly, but it was the solution that we were looking for and it was brought to me on a plate by an engineer who had nothing to do with security. This is a perfect illustration of the benefits of being open-minded and candid with your peers. If you will be making the ultimate decision, decide only when you have heard all the other options. Question your team if they come with ideas different from yours. They may have already faced an identical or similar problem. I often say that a pessimist is an optimist with experience. But all experience need not be negative; some of your colleagues may have faced problems and used solutions that you never thought about. Be open-minded, and avoid the hierarchy complex. Just because you are the boss does not mean that you are right. You are the boss because you have an open mind, are able to listen to what others have to say, and can change your mind if a better solution suddenly becomes available. It requires intelligence, humility, and character to accept that a subordinate can come up with a better idea than yours. But it should not surprise you. Remember you are a manager, not a specialist. You probably have not faced all the issues that your subordinates have faced, altogether, in their career. And a different point of view should not be taken personally. It should be listened to and discussed in an open conversation, where all feel like valuable contributors. This does not change the fact that the final decision should be yours and that, once taken, you accept full responsibility for it! Remember: to accept responsibility is to be in control.

THE STANDARD APPROACH TO PROBLEM SOLVING AND THE SYSTEMATIC METHOD

I borrow this standard approach to problem solving from Dobbins and Pettman (2006: 13), but I guess it is a well-known approach taught in many business schools. Five steps are suggested.

1. Define the Problem with Great Clarity
It is crucial to put the problem at hand at the center of your thinking process and to establish clearly what it consists of. Your problem becomes your target challenge because every issue must create a target-centric attitude. Once you have defined the problem with as much clarity as possible, this problem becomes your target and your thinking, your creativity, and your actions will automatically become target centered. Define the problem in writing and make it a challenge to be solved.

2. Collect Information
You need to put all the facts, actors, problems, and hurdles in writing to collect as much information as possible about the target question. You must do so in some sort of detached way. Do not frown, or moan or groan. Just list facts with a smile on your face. You will be surprised at how it can impact finding a solution. Do not take anything personally, and separate people from the issue at hand. You and your team must focus on the problem/challenge and its solution. Be target-centric in your collection of data. Keep to the task you have to solve and only to it. This does not mean that you must not carry on keeping an open mind and remain curious about what surrounds you, but for the data collection you must stay focused. Collect enough data to help with answering these questions:

- What does the management want as a solution?
- Is it our preferred solution?
- Is it really the perfect outcome?

175

- What consequences would follow if we follow management's advice?
- What exactly are we trying to achieve and isn't there a better way to reach this perfect outcome?
- Does the outcome satisfy the needs and objectives we have in mind, does it fit the budget, and will it make the management happy?
- Will they support the solution even if it is not what they had in mind initially?
- Is there a better way to achieve a similar outcome? Are there better alternatives?
- How biased are we and are our assumptions reasonable?
- What about others who may have faced the same issues (in the organization, in the industry, in an affiliate abroad, etc.)?
- Apply the three Ts! (think, think, and think)

3. Ask Others for Advice

As demonstrated in the solar panel story, others that belong to your inner circle but are not necessarily security people may have your solution at the ready and be, of course, totally unaware that it is needed. Without betraying secrets, discuss your problems with peers and colleagues. Belonging to an association such as the local chapter of ASIS International, OSAC, or the Security Institute can prove very valuable. People you meet there usually have vast experience. They may not be directly related to your industry, but they are ready to help and may provide insightful suggestions that could steer you toward the right solution. You must be able to tap into the knowledge, the skills, the experience, and the imagination of others. Do not feel above asking for help. Do not think you show weakness or incompetence by discussing your problems. Security people usually love talking about security issues and are always willing to offer interesting solutions. Although many would not consider themselves to be creative people, I think that they often display an amazing amount of creativity and original thinking. Furthermore, security practitioners are usually willing to help. Ask for help, and it will probably be given.

4. First Try to Find the Conscious Solution, Then Ask the Subconscious for Help

Dobbins and Pettman suggest that if you cannot find an obvious solution, you should "feed all the information into the subconscious/superconscious sections of the [brain]" (Dobbins and Pettman 2006: 14). Michalko has the same advice and provides a model of action to activate the subconscious (Michalko 2011). Serious research has proven that there is something unquestionable about the power of the subconscious and one must tap into this reservoir, which is there, at your service, and just needs to be prompted.

In the previous chapter, we discussed mental laws and how they can help you reach any solution. In his seminal book *Creative Thinkering*, Michalko proposes a *thought experiment* that I reproduce here verbatim. It illustrates many of the mental laws exposed in the previous chapter and serves as an application of the systematic method described above.

> Work on a problem until you have mulled over all the relevant pieces of information. Talk with others about the problem, ask questions, and do as much research as you can until you are satisfied that you have pushed your conscious mind to its limit. Write a letter to your unconscious mind about the problem. Make the letter as detailed and specific as possible. Define the problem, describe its attributes, what steps you have taken, the difficulties, the gaps, what is needed, what you want, and so on. Just writing the letter will help better define the problem, clarify issues, point out where more information is needed and prepare you unconscious to work on a solution. The letter should read as if it were written to a real person. Imagine that your unconscious is all-knowing and can solve any problem that is properly stated. Instruct your unconscious to find the solution. Write: "your mission is to find the solution to the problem. I would like the solution in two days". Seal the letter and put it away. You may even want to mail it to yourself. Let go of the problem. Don't work on it. Forget it. Do something else. This is the incubation stage, when much of what goes on occurs outside your focused awareness, in your unconscious. Open the letter in two days. If the problem has not been solved, write on the bottom of the letter: "Let me know the minute you solve it," and put it away. Sooner or later, when you are most relaxed and removed from the problem, the answer will magically pop into your mind. (Michalko 2011: 137–138)

I am a firm believer in the power of the subconscious and can recount countless experiences where solutions to apparently unsolvable problems were found after a solitary run or a long walk by the sea.

5. Be Ready for a Revelation

If the problem at hand seems difficult to solve, you will need to focus and concentrate on its possible solutions. If the solution to reach the best outcome does not reveal itself, go through the problem, the available information, the obvious hurdles, the assumptions, and so on and mentally rehearse all these elements before going to bed. Ask your subconscious for a precise solution. If nothing happens, insist. Go for a walk, a run, a game of golf, or practice your favorite sport—anything that keeps your body busy and lets your brain focus on a first-level, physical activity. Your superconscious will have time to think for you and will provide a solution. But beware, the solution will probably come at a moment that you do not expect. Keep a piece of paper and a pencil close by or use your phone to record the solution. It will often come at a funny time and will not be in print. You must seize the moment or it will be gone and the solution with it, like a dream. I have gotten in the habit of doing this for more than solutions and any new idea I have, I use my iPhone Recording app. If I am driving, I have this app in my favorites and just need to put my finger on the arrow and then explain what I have in mind.

PRINCIPLES OF BRAINSTORMING AND THE SYSTEMATIC METHOD

The systematic method encompasses the traditional SWOT analysis (Strengths, Weaknesses Opportunities and Threats) in a less formal, rigid way. It is a very simply put ten-stage approach to problem solving. It starts with posing the problem in very specific ways, a bit like creating a KPI. The target question, as I will call it, must be specific and if possible comprise figures such as an expected result with a related deadline. For example, how, with the current workforce, can we ensure the protection of our new headquarters in town when the building is completed by August 2019? While it seems at first impossible that the same number of security officers can cover an extra building, the management is adamant that the 2019 budget will not provide for an increase in the number of personnel. This kind of requirement is faced almost every year by security managers: *do more with less!*

The systematic method (Dobbins and Pettman 2006: 16) suggests the following:

1. You must first assume that there is a workable solution and expect that you and your team will find the best possible solution.
2. Use positive language in your thoughts but also in your dealings with your staff. Avoid the bad military habit of blaming the

hierarchy for forcing you into unrealistic things and thinking that only you and your team will pay the price. This is negative and negative feelings have no place in your new attitude. Blaming others is losing control. You are now in control; you take responsibility and you do not blame others.

3. Define the situation with great clarity. Do not forget that establishing the problem clearly is already solving 50% of it. Brainstorm with your people, and use flipcharts or whiteboards. Put things in writing. *Verba volant, scripta manent.*

4. Identify all causes of the problem. Which can be passed over and which seem overwhelming? Do not look for solutions right now. Just make a list of everything that stands between now and the perfect outcome.

5. Make a list of all the possible solutions. Not only the obvious ones, but all that are possible. For this I suggest that you use the 20-idea mindstorming technique. Of course, if you are on your own, it will be more difficult, and the most difficult thing will be to isolate yourself with the whiteboard or the flipchart and work on it.

6. Establish a deadline for your decision. Making a decision is good provided it is timely. You must find a solution before a certain date to have enough time to implement your strategy. Establishing a deadline will help you and your team focus on the outcome. Mental laws will help you fine-tune the solution by the date you have decided to act.

7. If you are the great responsible, you cannot do everything. Assign responsibility to your team members, according to their level and their capability. Empower them, but do it wisely. I remember a security manager who asked security officers to do some training online and report the results to him. This would have been acceptable if the type and nature of training would have been related to a security need in their enterprise, but this does not seem to have been the case. Security officers ended up taking a lot of short certifications that they thought looked good on their resumes, but did not really improve the security posture of the company. You are in charge, you are in control, you assign responsibility. You monitor the progress of the individuals tasked with actions, you help them think, and you guide them when they feel unsure. But action has to be taken.

8. If there is deadline for deciding on a course of action, there must also be a deadline for the complete realization of the task. This deadline must be realistic in order to avoid unwanted stress on the team.

9. Once the deadline is known, reverse the timeline and specify dates by which actions need to be completed. A Gantt chart does that well, but I, for example, am deplorable at using Gantt charts. One of your officers may be good at that. Use all available skills to reach the goals. Otherwise, draw a simple table with Word. There is no shame in doing this.

10. What gets measured gets done. And what does not get measured will probably never come into being. Once you have assigned responsibilities to your people, you must review their progress, regularly. If you like working with percentages, track percentage of completion. I do not like doing this because people feel obliged to add a few points weekly to what they do, even if they have done nothing. Somehow it encourages cheating. This is not fair and this is not a mature attitude. But find a way to measure what your team members are doing, and make sure that they are not going around in circles. You are there to put them back on track and make them move forward. You are accountable more than they are!

CPTED AND BEYOND

Crime prevention through environmental design is a very creative way of addressing security issues. Several major books have been written about CPTED, and they are cited in the references.

CPTED works according to a number of principles. These principles are simple and straightforward. The purpose of CPTED is primarily to give the space back to its legitimate owners. It is in the means and ways of doing that CPTED (pronounced Cep-Ted) appeals to creativity. CPTED has its origins in architecture and this is probably why it took some time to be fully accepted by law enforcement agencies. Nowadays, these agencies, particularly in the United States, are at the forefront of CPTED applications. The strength of CPTED is to propose ready-to-go designs that will save time for the security consultant or manager. Let us first discuss the main principles that make CPTED a fantastic tool for security executives.

We will then see other ways to add to these principles to reach an original and creative security program for your facility.

CPTED Principles

The idea behind crime prevention through environmental design is that "the physical environment can be manipulated to produce behavioural effects that will reduce the incidence and fear of crime, thereby improving the quality of life" (Crowe 2000: 35). This is not a new idea. As Crowe aptly cites, the idea behind Napoleon III's redesign of the main Parisian arteries was motivated partly by the need to produce great works to keep the population under control while simultaneously authorizing his chief of police "to raze or demolish any building or habitat know to be the hideout of criminals" (2000: 87) in the nineteenth-century capital. But it is really in the twentieth century that CPTED became a full approach to environment and architectural design. My purpose here is not to reproduce or duplicate the work of authors who have really perfectly summarised what CPTED is (Crowe 2000 and Atlas 2008) but to establish a relation between CPTED and creativity. I am not really interested in the impact of CPTED since it has been amply demonstrated. My approach is more about aesthetics and beautification, and how a creative mind can improve this part of CPTED. CPTED uses the environment to affect human behavior. It uses creativity to encourage some behaviors and try to discourage others. It does that through changes in the environment that speak to the human senses and trigger human reaction that can be anticipated. One example: if you want drivers to slow down at a particular point, using paving stones instead of tarmac is always the solution. Because of their irregular surface, they increase the noise and vibrations in the car, which naturally will make the driver release the pedal and adopt a lower speed. The cobbled area therefore speaks to the senses, the view because it usually is of a different color—using red cobbles will have the subliminal impact of linking the color with red that means stop. Crowe aptly remarks on how colors affect behaviour.

> Some behavioural responses are learned, such as responses to red and green lights. Blue police uniforms cause socialized responses that we tend to associate with authority. People pass the time less well in red. Red leads to increased blood pressure, respiratory rate, and eye blink frequency. Blue has the opposite effect. (Crowe 2000: 104)

CPTED therefore use the subconscious and subliminal impact of the environment to create feelings of comfort (or discomfort) that will, in turn,

181

generate behaviors. CPTED is based on strategies that are well known today: natural access control, natural surveillance, and territorial reinforcement. The notion of designing space to modify behavior is fascinating and a definite breakthrough in physical security theory, and I encourage all security practitioners to at least familiarize themselves with the principles of CPTED. What first really attracted me to this approach was the modification of environment through natural-looking features that really impact behaviors. In the region where I have been working for two decades, beautification is very common. Old administrative buildings, parks, and office buildings regularly undergo beautification transformations, and I believe it is at the juncture of beautification and security that creativity should really be applied.

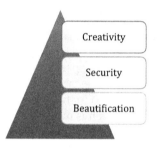

CPTED practitioners have worked very hard to determine the stimuli created by specific features in the environment and how they affect people's behavior. It does not mean that they ignore traditional security. As Crowe aptly remarks, "The CPTED planner tries to maximize the use of natural strategies before using the costliest organized and mechanical one that may actually serve as impediments to profitable operations" (Crowe 2000: 51). This cognitive approach can be resumed here in a few words.

Creative Thinking Beyond CPTED

Dean Keist Simonton, a psychologist, observed that creative thinking demands the ability to make novel combinations. If you examine most ideas, you will discover that they are the combination of two or more different elements and "It is the conceptual blending of dissimilar concepts that leads to original ideas and insights" (cited in Michalko 2011: 19).

If we want to go beyond CPTED as it is operating at the moment, we need to add a touch of creativity to our thinking. Few people would associate the world of corporate security with the idea of creativity. Most security practitioners do not envision their field of competence as one where creativity is necessary and they tend to see creativity and competence as opposing concepts. Although some say that security is an art, security practitioners do not perceive themselves as artists. They see themselves as methodical, rigorous professionals whose job rests on a mix of discipline, methodology, and experience. Often with police or military backgrounds, their creative talent was seldom encouraged during the first career. It may even have been frowned upon past the rank of second lieutenant, which is sad because creativity has a role to play in security. Creativity must be seen as a means to make security, and more particularly physical security, less conspicuous, less aggressive, and more effective. Creative security envisions not a world where fences are put down, or became invisible, but a world where fences seem to perform another mission and security professionals may look like business people or hotel clerks. Based on principles developed by the CPTED philosophy, creative security concentrates on the psychological impact of security design on the criminal mind but also on the mind of honest people. Its principles are many, but they are all driven by the idea that security requirements must be answered but not seen, transformed from their original brutal nature to some kind of peaceful and harmonious design. Some kind of feng shui approach to security?

I like to retell this story although it is a very old reminiscence and I cannot ensure it was like this. This is simply how it registered in my brain. I lived for 17 years in Pretoria, the jacaranda city and capital of South Africa. When driving from Pretoria, on the N1 South toward Johannesburg, there was and still is today on the eastern side of the highway a modern circular building set up in a beautifully landscaped garden. I will not name this iconic building which is well-known to most Gautengers.[1] I do not think that this is still the case today but a couple of decades back, several antelopes—I think they were springboks, but they might have been impalas—roamed the landscaped garden around the building all day long. There was, next to the meshed fence that was therefore visible to all motorists, a floodlit

183

waterhole, where these small antelopes came to drink, indifferent to the roaring of engines on the nearby highway for the greatest pleasure of motorists, and particularly of their young children. Of course, all South Africans are aware that a small antelope can clear easily 2.4 meters in height and to make sure that they did not escape the safety of the park, a 3-meter-high chain link fence had been erected. Its chain link nature allowed everybody to see the antelopes and nobody would think about complaining about this fence. But maybe the main purpose of this fence surrounding this headquarters was to prevent trespassers from trying to defeat the security of the place and access the headquarters' business secrets. It could also be that the cameras monitoring the springboks could at the same time detect possible intruders. Furthermore, the whole area was absolutely unapproachable, since lighting covered large areas, as on a night-lit golf course. The area lighting was strong enough to illuminate and deter potential intruders. Under cover of a mini nature reserve, the security department had created a first-class setup where the perimeter fence was perceived as a game fence intent on protecting wild animals from being run down by reckless drivers on the highway, while it provided full visibility of the surroundings of the building, excellent lighting at night thanks to floodlit waterholes located at strategic points, and an extraordinary number of security wardens, the thousands of drivers and their young passengers driving on this highway who gazed intently toward the fence, in the hope of spotting antelopes, acting, unintentionally as little security wardens, ensuring the place's integrity. There was not a commercial fence in the world equipped with so many pairs of private eyes scrutinizing it on a 24/7 basis!

This was the most fascinating example of creative thinking in security I have ever seen. It was a combination of garden landscaping (CPTED) combined with the idea of a mini game reserve (creative thinking)—two concepts seldom associated offered a remarkable natural surveillance opportunity. Although I have tried my best to think of other examples and suggestions regarding applied creative thinking in security, I always come back to this one. Everything is there: the security requirements, perimeter security, surveillance, anti-intrusion system, and so on. And none of it appears to be what it is. The security function was hidden behind beautiful and appeasing surroundings and natural surveillance—CPTED extended to its maximum capability. The security manager enrolled hundred of unconscious wardens and their children to perform incessant surveillance. And the cost of it was almost nonexistent: Was this setup not creative security at its best?

This is what security managers should aim for. First blend security devices and features around beautiful surroundings, as much as possible. Use CPTED techniques to create awareness and generate unconscious behaviors, empower employees, and always try to improve the surroundings. Plant trees if you can, but trees with a tactical position; create ponds in areas that cannot be controlled; and illuminate places when you can, but illuminate for a reason. You must think permanently along those lines: make security unobtrusive and embellish the surroundings. Use hard physical security only when you really have no other choice. And even then, think about how to make bollards bearable, perhaps by transforming them into chairs or benches. Blend them into the landscape. Twist nature's arm to make it fit your security needs. People will appreciate surroundings that they find pleasant and attractive. Use natural surveillance, and change the design, create landscaped gardens, and train both your security officers and the organization's other employees. By simply moving a few tons of ground, you can achieve security miracles and effective physical security that does not look like security. Never forget that security often irritates. Who likes going through security at airports? No one, anywhere. Make security imaginative and handsome, and people will go for it. Human beings love beautiful things.

SUMMARY

In this chapter, we have discussed the possible relationship between security and creativity. We have highlighted some of the components of creativity and hopefully demonstrated that security can, and even should, be creative if it wants to alter its poor image. To that effect, I suggested a problem-solving method to help security managers use their creativity in the service of security. I then discussed briefly how the principles of CPTED could be a gateway to more creative physical security and how creativity should become, whenever possible, the preferred approach to finding solutions to security challenges.

MAIN POINTS

- There is no reason why security cannot be creative. Creativity is about the ability to improve, so we should all be creative.
- Problem solving requires clarity. Being clear about a problem is already solving 50% of it!
- The systematic problem-solving method will help you solve security challenges while encouraging more creative approaches.
- Use the mental laws to your benefit. They are keys to your hidden, deep-set creativity and are there to serve you.
- CPTED is the first step toward creative physical security. Become familiar with it and all its principles and then, when you are ready, go beyond.
- Every training is specific and performance improves with exercise. The more you play with creative ideas and concepts, the more comfortable and effective you will become.
- Trust yourself, believe that you are a creative security manager, and be bold, and your creativity will develop.

END NOTE

1 The inhabitants of Gauteng, the province of South Africa that includes the two major cities of Pretoria and Johannesburg.

REFERENCES

Atlas, R. (2008) *21st Century Security and CPTED: Designing for Critical Infrastructure Protection and Crime Prevention.* CRC Press: Boca Raton, FL.

Crowe, T. D. (2000) *Crime Prevention Through Environmental Design: Applications of Architectural Design and Space Management Concepts,* 2nd ed. National Crime Prevention Institute: London, UK.

Dobbins, R. & Pettman, B. O. (2006) *What Self-Made Millionaires Really Think, Know and Do: A Straight-Talking Guide to Business Success and Personal Riches.* Capstone: Chichester, UK.

Michalko, M. (2011) *Creative Thinkering: Putting your Imagination to Work.* New World Library: Novato, CA.

8

Summary

Chapter 8 will be a short conclusion and summary chapter, a synthesis of the ideas advanced in this book and of the ways to implement some of the recommendations made for the benefit of the organization and of the security practitioner.

BEFORE WE WRAP UP...

"Tell them what you are going to tell them, tell them, and then tell them what you just told them." Everyone knows this old formula, and the purpose of this chapter is very close to that. This is not a bad idea, providing you do not repeat verbatim what you told them. It is good sometimes to emphasize.

In this book, I have tried to work on a two-pronged approach. On the one hand I wanted to help the security manager approach her task as a security executive to the best of her ability and with solid guidelines in mind. Second I wanted to give security managers the tools to help them promote themselves as individuals and to make them feel valuable, effective, and ready to move up the next step on the corporate ladder. I do not know if the result is what I wanted this book to be. I have put a lot of my own experience in these chapters and hope this experience will be helpful. Usually, the experience of others is not. One needs to learn from one's own mistakes. But others' experience may help anticipate a failure or a wrong move.

Chapter 1 introduced the topic of strategic thinking in a corporate environment. Understanding what a strategy is and how it should be implemented is not in itself ground-breaking. What I think brings some salt to the chapter is the importance of the cultural aspect of strategy. As everyone knows, organizations develop their own cultures with time. This is true for relatively homogenous organizations—I mean homogenous in terms of the population composing the workforce—but also applies to multicultural organizations. Multicultural organizations are entities where the management and the workforce are composed of individuals that do not share the same cultures and values. It really takes a lot of effort to create a company culture when the individuals who compose the workforce come from vastly different backgrounds. However, I worked at a company in the GCC which achieved just that. It managed, in spite of an extremely disparate workforce, to create a spirit of seriousness and to maintain compliance to standards and politically correct attitudes in all fields. This worked well and everybody was reasonably happy sharing this new culture until the human material became more homogenous, creating strata of responsibilities aligned along nationality lines. With this development, the sentiment of justice started to deteriorate and I do not know how the situation evolved since I left the company quite some time ago. This did not come as a surprise since the idea behind the creation of this company was, apart from making profits, to provide employment for the locals. Foreigners were hired to bring the know-how and the expertise and once these two elements were transferred to the locals, there was no point in carrying on as before. Yet, it was a very interesting experience for a security practitioner and I really enjoyed the 4 years I spent on that job. What was extremely interesting is that during the international period of the organization the two-thirds year of the project phase, best practice was the norm, even in terms of security. The security team, led by myself, was a multinational force with Americans, North and South Africans, and Filipinos, and everyone wanted to deliver the best possible security service. The war in Iraq was at its peak then, terrorist attacks in KSA were just abating, and security cadres studied the different attack scenarios occurring in the region and tried to anticipate problems and find solutions should such attacks occur in our area while preparing the security elements for the worst. Yet, when the project phase ended, locals started to run the show with a more parochial approach, and the level of security started to dive to a very low level, partly as a consequence of policies of financial rationalization. The guard force I had recruited was replaced by a supermarket security guard force from a country where labor sells very cheap, European and American cadres were thanked for their service on their way out the door, and best practices were ignored almost overnight. Anything that hampered the movements and the well-being of the locals was discarded forthwith and security became what it should never have been. The choices made in that sense were logical, after all, since the management never believed in threats. After all, it is all about perception and their perception was correct. To my knowledge, this organization has not suffered any attacks since I left them a decade ago. The purpose of this digression is to highlight the importance of culture, or cultures (plural). You will not be able to go against culture, and it is best to be aware of this when you accept a job.

In Chapter 2, I discussed the issue of credibility that most security managers face when it comes to the decision-making level. I considered both the case of the proprietary security manager, employed by the organization and traditionally reporting to a VP of security or chief security officer, and the case of the security consultant deployed to protect a group of expatriate workers in volatile environments. Both these security practitioners often have to face opposition from both the employees they are supposed to protect, who reluctantly accept the constraints of security, and from the management, which either finds the threats advanced by their security manager ludicrous, thereby denying credibility (and budget) for the security department outside of basic requirements (guard force, vehicles, a basic CCTV operation, and a symbolic access control system), or tries to transfer their responsibility for decisions toward the security manager in case of crisis, emergency, or the need to trigger an evacuation plan (which is rarely the case, as the security manager or consultant most of the time works in an advisory capacity).

In this chapter, I also discussed the expectations of the executive management toward the security professionals working for them—what they should be, what they often are in reality—and I mentioned the snares the security manager should expect and try to avoid.

In Chapter 3, I suggested that new security executives begin their assignment by tackling a new (or updated) security master plan for the organization they are tasked with protecting. I proposed content found in most security master plans and discussed the issue of the limits of the plan. There is always a potential scope creep to any SMP, particularly if this is a new one. Limits must be clearly established in the preface of the plan.

What you, as a security practitioner, should consider is where you want to establish the limits. You should ask yourself the right questions:

- Do you want to extend security to the business security plan?
- An emergency and crisis management plan?
- An evacuation plan, a business continuity plan?
- Do you have the capability to do all these plans on your own?
- Have you got the relevant experience and writing skills in your team?
- Will you have to hire a specialist to do the job?

This issue is of course crucial since, most of the time, security department budgets are tight and turning to external specialists, particularly when you have just been appointed, is frowned upon. Try to do the best possible work with the skills you can muster inside your team. There are competencies that can be profitable for the department and the whole workforce. You may want to consider more than a simple security plan: What about a cyber security plan? If you have a good relationship with the IT department manager, you may want to come to an agreement with the IT manager to create a specific IT and information procedure that will include both physical security information protection as well as IT regulations. The relationship with IT regarding the protection of the organization is an important issue that I never managed satisfactorily.

I then discussed change and how it should be fought for. A new security manager will always bring changes in security processes and these changes will seldom be welcomed by the workforce. How to plan and prioritize these changes was discussed, as well as the necessity—or not—of involving employees through consultations and/or awareness programs. Security executives must be good at understanding the management of change. They must understand it, plan for it, and anticipate the inevitable resistance it will generate. Security managers must, along with their team, be able to understand which changes are crucial, and which changes will be accepted more willingly than others. I discussed how security executives must work on how to bring this change, by understanding who their allies are and who will probably fight a rearguard battle.

I have highlighted the need to consult with employees, but perhaps I did not emphasize enough how difficult it can be sometimes. If you belong to a small organization, this is quite doable, but if you work for a major company, reaching employees becomes difficult. There are number of reasons for that. First, if you want to reach them all, this can be done only through the intranet and/or any internal communication systems that is available in your organization. Yet, for an unfathomable reason, senior management do not like to see security messages on the intranet. As if making people aware of security issues makes these security issues more probable. The policy of burying one's head in the sand seems a favored strategy in some—many?—organizations. I was told repeatedly that security awareness was scaring people and that since "where there is smoke there is fire," employees were prone to assume that "if the security department is speaking to us, it is because we are under threat." You may also face a managerial issue, one I faced at some stage in my career. I was asked once to minimize the threat to avoid demands for salary increases. In 2004, I was in charge of the security of a number of expatriates in one of the sheikdoms of the GCC. The expatriate workers were driving every morning to a place of work and had to go through areas known for their radical population. Some time into my assignment, I was asked to do a presentation to a team of managers coming from headquarters in Europe and one of the slides was highlighting the specific dangers of the area in question. I mentioned that orders had been given to the workers to drive in convoy in order to be able to collect their colleagues in case of a flat tire, for example. Not that I thought that a flat tire would have triggered a dangerous attack from the local inhabitants, but just to be on the safe side. My colleague and I would have driven down to the place and changed the tire. I was pretty confident that the danger was marginal but wanted to show the delegation that we really did the best we could to protect their employees. During the presentation, I could see that the audience was not reacting positively to my explanations. Before I had even finished the presentation, one of the delegates asked me, "Has anybody seen this presentation?" I replied that this presentation had been prepared for them and that nobody else had seen it so far. To my negative reply, he pursued: "In that case, suppress this slide about the route between the compounds and the place of work." I was surprised and told the group that this was a serious issue and that they had to be aware that we had a potential security problem at this point. The reply was simple: "There is no other route available, and therefore we cannot do anything, am I correct?" I replied that we had already taken all common-sense measures to make sure that the risk was minimized and that we could not really do better in the circumstances. He replied that if the employees learned of such danger, they would probably demand a risk premium that the company was not ready to give. Second, if there was an attack and it was proved that the HQ had been made aware of a potential risk, trade unions and/or victims would probably sue the organization at home, and subsequent financial consequences would be certain. It was quite straightforward and I saw their point, but the onus was on us to determine where the risk was real and how it could be minimized. I told them that it was impossible for me to tell them that this portion of the route was risk free and that we were paid to measure the risk and propose mitigation measures, which was what we had done with the means at our disposal. Tension was palpable in the room. The visitors did not insist but once back home, made a very nasty report on our attitude with the result that the consultancy that employed us had to bow to their demands. The purpose of this example is simply to underline the fact that security is seldom popular even among those it is supposed to serve. It is a tolerated department and the quieter it stays, the better it is for everybody. This is why security awareness, if it looks great on paper, is rarely implemented. It frightens people, or at least those in management. Is it justified and what would happen if security practitioners did perform security awareness sessions on a regular basis to the workforce? In all honesty, I do not know. Although I have written many security awareness programs, I never implemented a single one. I thought it was just circumstances that prevented me from doing so, but recently discussing the point with a fellow practitioner, he told me that his experience with awareness programs had been very comparable to mine. Yet, another younger colleague of mine who worked for a major French pharmaceutical company shared his experience with me that confirmed that some organizations "go for it."

The solution might rest with the consultation of employees in the elaboration of the program. The topic being so sensitive, it may be a good idea to have nonspecialist perspectives to build the program. Should this be the case, I suggest that you keep a leading role in the preparation, because you are the one who knows what awareness should cover. Keep the lead and listen to employees—and middle level managers—if only in order to find a palatable way to convey your message. Do not give in on the essentials. Accept changes to the shape of the implementation. As discussed, each action creates a reaction and change in the execution of a new security philosophy will definitely generate resistance. If it does not, start questioning the validity and reality of the suggested changes! I call this resistance *friction* when it is active. It is people refusing to abide by a new rule, for example, like refusing to park according to a new system that works to their disadvantage. People, in things that affect them in their daily comfort at work, might be vocal to a level that may sometimes reach the level of minor workplace violence (often in the form of verbal abuse toward the security workforce). This type of incident is quite easy to prevent through discipline. Senior management cannot tolerate unruly behaviour and such incidents will be few, and sanctions (or at least warning from hierarchy) are normally sufficient. The more traditional reaction to security change will be passive resistance, which you and your team cannot immediately visualize and which is somewhat more difficult to fight.

An attrition battle normally begins and a lot of diplomacy and patience will be necessary to reach acceptance. This is where you need to keep a balance between information and retribution. Start with explaining why the changes are needed and why new rules have to be implemented. Use the means at your disposal. If your company edits a magazine or a monthly newsletter, ask the editor (nicely) to keep a bit of space for you and use that space to do a bit of security awareness. Petty tampering with access control, badges, and unruly visitors left to themselves in corridors are just bad habits that will be easily corrected, because employees are somehow conscious that they should not exist. A bit of discipline will—surprisingly—sometimes be even welcome.

Consider the resistance to change as your biggest challenge in the implementation of the security program. It is there that your mettle will be tested, both by your hierarchy and by the workforce. This is really the stage where you cannot fail, and your department must also be aware of the consequences of failure. The way you have anticipated change and how you implement it are crucial to your image and status in the company. I do not mean that succeeding will gain you promotion. Being promoted does not work very well in security. Sadly, you will have to use your success as a way to get the next job, with more responsibilities and a better salary.

Chapter 4 dealt essentially with metrics and the measurements of security. Like most security practitioners, I know how difficult it can be to justify my actions—and my requests—to my hierarchy. I have observed in the corporate context how financiers, HR people, and even safety personnel bombard the upper management with documents full of charts, pies, and columns and at first, willing to emulate them, I found it almost impossible to find things that would demonstrate the positive impact of my work on the security posture of the company. I read everything I could about metrics, and even then, I did not see eye to eye with many metrics authors. I was not happy with examples provided, because I tried to adopt the CEO's perspective, and providing columns of visitors, incidents, and the like did not appear to me convincing and seriously lacked the gravitas expected from senior managers. With time, I managed to put together a number of metrics that "meant something in terms of management." These are the metrics I suggest in Chapter 4. During a course in performance management offered by a reputable company in Dubai, I was introduced to three performance criteria that I also described: critical success factors (CSF), key results areas (KRAs), and key performance indicators (KPIs). This was an eye opener and I still today consider these three concepts crucial to goal setting for a security department. This chapter is important because it really provides a thinking framework to place your actions as a security executive within limits and shows convincingly, I hope, how to develop a program that will definitely enhance the security posture of the company placed under your protection. Of course, it illustrates the old adage that "to get done, any action needs to get measured."

Many clients I have worked with in the last 20 years have some kind of fascination with KPI, probably because the association of the three words, *key*, *performance*, and *indicator*, look like a miracle equation that sums it all up! I hope I have explained clearly that KPIs are only the last stage of a process that needs to be guided by reflection and be in line with the business objectives of the organization. Usually when you do not antagonize your client and present your work according to CSFs, KRAs, and KPIs, the work is appreciated.

In Chapter 5, I discussed the very important issue of the maintenance of the security program and one of its main components, security awareness. These are two very important issues that will keep you and your team busy once the initial program has been fully implemented. In the chapter, I suggested ideas for the awareness program but there are no limits to what you can conceive. The limits sit in the C-suite and how your hierarchy perceives security at this precise moment. Surprisingly, or maybe not so surprisingly, it is when the threat seems to come closer that the management adopts a negative attitude toward awareness. When the threat seems far off, you can organize security awareness sessions for families in compounds with tea and scones without too many complications. When the atmosphere tenses, these sessions are perceived as bad for morale and should be avoided. For us security practitioners, it does not make any sense, but for top managers, it does. A looming threat means more risk, and it means a deteriorating working atmosphere. It can mean security bonuses paid for risk acceptance, and it finally means, in the case of a workforce deployed with families and children, making the decision to repatriate spouses and children with the enormous cost of compounds suddenly empty (compounds that sometimes have been paid a year in advance), schools deserted (something the local ambassador usually disapproves of), and so on. When the threat increases, the management wants the crisis to be suddenly treated with the utmost discretion and to avoid at all cost scaring families. I could measure, during a recent assignment in East Asia, how such tension impacts the atmosphere in the workplace. In this case, the preparation of an evacuation plan, and the consultation of all employees concerned, was enough to restore some confidence in the management and was the right decision (taken by the HQ in Europe). Action always beats inertia!

Training is of course an important point, and like in the military, it must be permanent. Security training must be balanced, a mix of instruction and practical training. Training a guard force could be a full-time job for one of your team members. Nothing is more important for the morale of a security officer than this feeling of being looked after granted by every training. In training, the security officer is the focus of everything. He is important, he is trained to become a better officer. If money is scarce, organize the training yourself. Use every opportunity to create some training, even walk through–talk through training sessions are effective. Take advantage of safety training, which is usually much easier to finance than security courses, for an unfathomable reason. Make your men and women basic firefighters or train them in CPR, first aid, defibrillator use… Train them, empower them, and show that you care!

I do not know if I emphasized enough the necessity of maintaining the security program with discipline and steadfastness. Many people in this world start things, but only a tiny fraction of them complete those things. And maintenance of security is about just that: keeping what you have started successful and relevant at all times. This is a much more complicated task than it first appears. But I would say that with training, this is what will really make the difference between a standard security manager and an outstanding one.

Security audits are another part of the maintenance program. As you can guess, maintaining the program while training your security force to a decent level is a very time-consuming activity. Planning is needed. The idea that security is a well-organized department is often strange to the upper management who sees security mainly as a bunch of people available in case of emergency, the rest of their time being spent sitting languidly at reception or walking unhurriedly in the corridors during working hours. This perception should be changed. This is why you must inform your hierarchy of these maintenance activities, awareness, training, and audits long in advance. Your superior, through these weekly/monthly reports, should come to realize that security is managed and does things. Who knows? It might help you get a new line of budget for training courses your men and women desperately crave.

Until Chapter 6, I spoke mainly about strategic thinking in the work context. But Chapter 6 breaks this logic and takes the reader in an unexpected direction. Strategic thinking can have a more personal application. Security practitioners operating in a corporate context also need to care for themselves. Like soldiers, they are taken for granted. It should not be so. I have written this chapter because I have noticed, in a long and varied career, that the best people do not often get the career they deserve. When I was a young subaltern in a paratrooper regiment, I believed that this lack of acknowledgement for the best and most dedicated officers was unfair, although, in retrospect, there was some kind of logic in the military career advancement scheme, but I was surprised to see that the same applied in the professional civilian world. Of course, reasons for a lack of advancement or promotion are multiple, and can be linked to your handsomeness, the social connections of your spouse, your name, your ethnic origins, and many other criteria that do vary with time and have been studied by social psychologists for decades. I also firmly came to believe that another reason was that security professionals lacked self-confidence in their capabilities and showed serious shortcomings when it came to promoting themselves. I appreciate that many of the factors that contribute to promotion cannot be helped, but I believe in self-development and I also trust that one can overcome social and/or physical impairments and still succeed in what they are doing. I am not a psychologist, and do not pretend to be one, but psychologists have written so many books on self-development—some made a fortune out of them—that I came to trust what they all agree upon. After all, nothing irritates a security practitioner more than when business people doubt their advice. So, trust the pros.

I discovered self-development very late in my professional career, and probably a bit too late to measure its promised effectiveness. Giving oneself goals, writing them down, visualizing, affirming, emotionalizing, and so on are more or less common recommendations from all these successful writers. They usually arrange them in different sequences, and insist on some aspects more than others, but they have a common framework that I believe is useful for career promotion. These books will help you focus on what you are doing and give you a guideline to move forward. I do not believe that you can be very good at something if you are just working daily on your chores. If this is what you do, you cannot have a feeling of fulfilment because what you are doing does not belong to an overarching plan, and leaves a feeling of emptiness, I am tempted to say of time wasted. Your daily work cannot be entirely satisfying if it is what keeps you busy and nothing else. You need goals that transcend you. These goals will feed the drives that lead, maybe not to riches, but to success, that is, the feeling of a satisfying and fulfilling life. In this chapter, I discussed the mental laws of success that you can, as an individual, use to your advantage. I have explained briefly what these laws and techniques are believed to be and how they can serve the individual. Psychologists have worked quite hard in the last 30 years on these ideas, many of them issued from neuro-linguistic programming and the work of Dale Carnegie and others and which have been promoted with success by the like of Jack Canfield. As I wrote previously, there is not much science in these laws, only reassuring principles that let you believe that if you set goals, and focus, you will inevitably reach these goals and fulfil your ambitions. This is only a pleasant thought and I think they should rather be seen as guidelines that will keep you focused on your professional and personal objectives. I might have discovered them too late in life to be able to check their promises, but at the end of the day, they help me live a happy professional and personal life and isn't that really what counts? The reason for their inclusion was mainly that I noticed a complete ignorance of principles of self-development with many of my colleagues in the security world and I thought they could all benefit from them.

There are two topics that I mentioned briefly and which, I think, should accompany security professionals in their careers. First is the issue of patience. Patience is said to be the mother of all virtues, and it is. It was Gandhi, I think, who said that "you should live as if you were to die tomorrow and learn as if you were to live forever." I like this quote and I have tried to apply it and continue to try. The security executive should be patient and patiently learn to become patient because impatience is a serious weakness. Everything you do in your job needs to be done with patience, at the correct pace, and in a timely manner. Success comes with work, effort, and time and time—alas—cannot really be compressed. We are told of successful youngsters and we know Marc Zuckerberg, Steve Jobs, and others, but there are not many like them, and they are certainly not made of the same mettle as we are. This book was not written for them, but for the regular security practitioner, a man or woman of many talents but perhaps not a genius?

A second topic I find interesting is assertiveness. As I write these words, I am still thinking about the advice I would like to give. I feel personally that I have lost one important job by lack of assertiveness, and that I kept one because of my low-profile attitude at the time. I know that being assertive is not being a bully, or being rude to others, but as Hadfield and Hasson observed, it is "about letting others know what you do and do not want in a confident and a direct way" (Hadfield and Hasson 2010: 7). This seems very fine, until you work in companies where the values are very different from yours. Americans, who cultivate assertiveness with success, are often perceived by non-Westerners as rude, brutal, and uncultured. I have often heard of people having difficulties dealing with South Asians that they found to be abrupt and arrogant, with very few diplomatic skills. Having worked for several internationally staffed organizations, I think that the issue of assertiveness needs to be given some thought by security practitioners. They may have to revise their attitudes and beliefs, and adopt a different attitude, one that reflect the values and beliefs of the workforce they have to work with every day. In some societies, kindness is associated with weakness, and assertiveness with aggressiveness. I believe that it is the cultural aspect that will define your approach toward assertiveness. It does not mean you should suddenly endorse wrong attitudes toward your management and your fellow workers. It simply means that you need to observe and try to understand what the values surrounding you are, and, from this observation, infer which behaviors to prefer to take you where you want to go. It is a very individual and personal decision, and you will have to work this out all alone.

What remains clear, and I would like to emphasize it again, is that you must take responsibility for your actions, wherever you are and whatever the culture you are bathing in, even if you are the only one to take responsibility. Never renege on this principle, because if you do and play the game of pointing fingers and blaming others, you will damage your self-esteem and confidence. This self-esteem is your main drive, it is what makes you move forward and therefore is your most important determinant. As Hadfield remarks, "confidence is your belief in your ability to do something. You need confidence to make decisions and take responsibility for what you say and do" (Hadfield 2010: 20). Because confidence is linked to responsibility and being responsible is being in control, you must never, ever default on this aspect of your personality. Let us give the last word to Lindenfield:

> "As adults, we must stand by our own values and judge ourselves by our own standards. Ultimately, our opinion of ourselves is the only one that matters" (Lindenfield 2014: 25).

My opinion is that more than being assertive, one needs to be courageous. Not the courage of the soldier facing action in the field, but the courage of the individual who makes decisions that can have an adverse impact on one's career and life. Being assertive in that sense is good. Being in control, taking responsibility, means that you will at some stage have to make decisions. You cannot always give the decision-making process to the hierarchy, because no decision will be made and the boat will never be rocked by anybody, because very few people in a position of authority want to leave their comfort zone. You may have to make decisions that you think need to be made and stand by them. One middle way is to inform your hierarchy about the decisions you are about to make. This is the wise move and it has the advantage of preparing your immediate superior to what is coming. And you may, if you are lucky, be given a green light, or a clear no-go. But my experience tells me that it is really when implementation is due to start that people start to think about your plan and will object to it. This is simply a fact of life. If you want things done, you will probably have to make decisions that may not be supported or endorsed by your hierarchy. But if you feel you have to make them, make them. Your self-esteem is what you need most in your professional career, and as long as you keep it at a satisfactory level, nothing, for you, will be entirely impossible.

To conclude, I would like to wish you good luck in your life. You may not always be in the world of industrial or corporate security, you may have unexpected encounters that will take you far from this profession, but for now, this is what feeds you and your family. As an individual of principles, you must do your job to the best of your abilities and in a way that satisfies the image that you have of yourself. I hope this book has helped you reflect on your place in a profession that is constantly adapting to new and often unexpected challenges. Be flexible, be courageous, and above all, be consistent.

This book, like any book with a vocational purpose, is a work in progress. If you have comments to make regarding ways to improve this book, do not hesitate to contact me through the editor. Because security changes and threats evolve continuously, some portions of this book will soon become obsolete. But in its broad lines, this is a book which should help you move forward, because you need to move forward. Because if you do not progress, you regress.

This should become some kind of motto for life. For life is action, not disorganized gesticulations. You must live a life with a purpose, and to fulfil this purpose, a plan should be made, even if life is unpredictable and circumstances do change. And it should be a plan that makes you a happy individual and a respected professional.

I sincerely hope this book will, in some modest way, provide some guidance, support, and direction as you plan strategically for your future.

REFERENCES

Hadfield, S. & Hasson, G. (2010) *How to Be Assertive in Any Situation*. Pearson: Harlow, UK.

Lindenfield, G. 3rd ed. (2014) *Assert Yourself: Simple Steps to Build your Confidence*. Harper Thornsons: London, UK.

INDEX

Note: Page numbers in italic and bold refer to figures and tables, respectively. Page numbers followed by n refer to footnotes.

Printed in the United States
by Baker & Taylor Publisher Services